The Warrior Bride

Prophetic Warfare Praise and Intimate Worship

Vanessa Richardson

The Warrior Bride

Vanessa Richardson can be contacted on:
bvrichardson@hotmail.com
and via
Liberation Ministries at
www.liberationministries.co.uk

Ip

Editing, design and layout by Life Publications
www.lifepublications.org.uk

Changing the spiritual atmosphere through the power of praise and worship to advance the Kingdom of God

The Warrior Bride

Acknowledgements

I am so thankful to God for so many wonderful people who, over the years, have encouraged me, stood with me, believed in me and the calling on my life.
I would like to thank in particular Chris Harnetty and Geoff Blease for proof reading and for their input into my book.
Also thanks to Liselle Appleby for the cover design and a big thank you to Dagmar Louw for the beautiful painting she did for the book cover, based on the scripture *Song of Songs 6:4 "Awesome as an army with banners"*.
Especially a BIG thank you to my husband Brian, who has stood with me, believed in me and tirelessly encouraged me to write this book.
And of course, my thanks to my heavenly Dad for His amazing love and faithfulness to me.

The Warrior Bride

Commendations

I have known Vanessa for over twenty years and this book is not a recent message, this has been a life message that she has carried ever since I have known her. She has always been passionate about intimacy with the Lord and has a great warfare anointing to see the kingdom of God expanded here on earth. As you read this book I am believing that you will become an intimate, passionate warrior of Christ as well.

Dr Sharon Stone
Founder and Senior Minister of
Christian International Europe

Warrior Bride is a tapestry that weaves together rich threads of biblical teaching, practical advice and valuable experience gleaned through the author leading worship nationally and internationally. This book should not only be read by experienced and aspiring worship leaders but by anyone serious about engaging with God in intimacy and depth.

John Glass
Former General Superintendent of Elim for sixteen years,
Chair of Council – Evangelical Alliance

I know of no one more able to write a book like this, born out of years of faithful courageous intimate worship and prophetic warfare praise. Vanessa inspires, encourages and educates us to capture the wind of heaven and shift spiritual atmospheres.

Rev Marilyn Harry
Elim Evangelist
Founder Love Wales

I have known Vanessa for eighteen years or so and over that time I have seen her mature and blossom, both as a person and as a powerful worship leader. My wife Jane, and I have been privileged to have Vanessa work alongside us at major breakthrough events where her ministry has brought a powerful presence of the Holy Spirit.

She has written this book from her heart. It is not theory but the practical lessons she has learned over many years of passionately pressing into the presence of God through music. I recommend everyone to read this book, especially those who lead in worship.

Rev Geoff Blease, Living Stones Ministries and
Regional Co-ordinator Metropolitan West Region
Elim Pentecostal Church

Contents

The Warrior Bride

Preface

God is calling us to higher heights and deeper depths with Him. This book gives vision and teaching to worshippers and worship leaders to rise up, flow with the movement of heaven, bring down the sounds of heaven, and to release heaven on earth through our praise and worship. We are called to change the spiritual atmosphere, bring breakthrough and pioneer new ground for the Gospel.

This book also gives some practical teaching on worship leading, song choice, the journey of worship, flowing in the spirit, activating spontaneous and prophetic worship, some biblical history of the music ministry, the requirements of a music minister, and the exhilaration of unfolding the truths of scripture in song.

The Warrior Bride

Introduction

It all began back in March 1984 when I surrendered my life to Jesus. Very soon after, I had a dream where God showed me very clearly that my calling was to the music ministry and in particular, to minister on the piano.

Since that time God has been so faithful to me. Initially I struggled so much in learning to play by ear, however, after months and months of fasting, praying and practicing, God began to break into my life and give me my own unique style on the piano.

I started out as second keyboard at Kensington Temple, then graduated to lead piano. It wasn't until I planted my own church with my dear friend Rev Soke Mun Ho in Wembley in 1992 that I started leading worship. In 1999 Brian, my husband, and I stepped out into our itinerant ministry, launching *Liberation Ministries*. Since then I have had the privilege of travelling the world, leading worship in conferences and churches not only in English, but also in French and Spanish. I still have a dream to lead worship in German.

I have enjoyed every nation, people group, language, culture, church and conference in which we have ministered, whether large or small. I have learnt so much and loved working with a great variety of musicians, singers and teams. I have also enjoyed teaching and mentoring several different worship teams and it has been a delight and privilege to watch them grow and develop.

My passion is to encourage worship teams to follow the Holy Spirit on the journey of worship into the heart of God and to flow in the prophetic anointing that God has given to us. The prophetic is our heritage and God desires all His music ministers to stir up the gift and flow with Him.

This book is written to encourage you on this journey. I want to hold up the dream that whatever your worship experience so far, there is so much more. It will take eternity to explore the mysteries of God!

I trust this book will encourage you to stretch your boundaries as you worship Him and lead others in worship.

Vanessa

1

The Warrior Bride

The Two-Fold Vision:

Prophetic Warfare Praise and Intimate Worship

O my love, you are as beautiful as Tirzah,
Lovely as Jerusalem,
Awesome as an army with banners!

Song of Songs 6:4

Many years ago, a friend, who had given me great encouragement, had a vision. She saw a beautiful bride dressed in a glorious wedding dress all ready and prepared to be married. The bride walked up the aisle towards her beloved and as she reached the top of the aisle, knelt with her future husband to pray, all could see that on her feet, instead of dainty wedding shoes were a pair of army boots!

What a beautiful picture of the church; the Warrior Bride. We are the Bride of Christ and God is preparing us for the Marriage of the Lamb, however, the church is in a battle. We have an enemy and we are called into the army of God to fight on behalf of those who do not yet know Christ and to fight for the church to be all that God intends for us; the beautiful, spotless, radiant and vibrant Bride of Christ.

There is a twofold vision

On the one hand God is calling us, His end time church, to rise up as an army and fight with all the weapons of warfare that He has given us. These weapons include the blood of Jesus Christ, the Word of God, our testimony, intercession and many more, but the weapon which I wish to focus on in this book is warfare praise and intimate worship.

On the other hand, we are the Bride of Christ called into intimacy with Him, our beloved Bridegroom. God is wooing us, His church, into an intimate relationship with Himself. Without this love relationship with Jesus it is much harder to sustain the battle. There is a limit to how long we can grit our teeth and fight without knowing His beautiful love surrounding us. A love that encourages us and calls us to follow Him ever more closely. We are called to partner with Jesus, the greatest lover of our souls, in the most exciting adventure of our lives!

> *My beloved spoke, and said to me: "Rise up,*
> *my love, my fair one, and come away."*

> *Song of Songs 2:10*

The High Praises

> *Let the high praises of God be in their mouth,*
> *And a two-edged sword in their hand,*
> *To execute vengeance on the nations,*
> *And punishments on the peoples;*
> *To bind their kings with chains,*
> *And their nobles with fetters of iron;*
> *To execute on them the written judgment –*
> *This honour have all His saints.*

> *Psalm 149:6-9*

Many years ago, God gave me a vision. He spoke to me from 2 Chronicles 20, the story of King Jehoshaphat.

This is a very well-known story from the Bible. King Jehoshaphat was the King of Judah and a very godly King. One day three great armies besieged Jerusalem with intent on its destruction. However, King Jehoshaphat called a fast. He called all the men, women, children and little ones to fast and to seek the Lord about the terrifying situation in which they found themselves.

The Bible tells us that the Spirit of God came upon one of the prophets who spoke to the people, saying: Thus says the Lord to you:

> *Do not be afraid nor dismayed because of this great multitude, for the battle is not yours, but God's.*
>
> *You will not need to fight in this battle. Position yourselves, stand still and see the salvation of the LORD, who is with you, O Judah and Jerusalem!*
>
> *2 Chronicles 20:15b, 17a*

The Bible tells us that the King received the word of the prophet and the next day he appointed singers and musicians to go out in front of the army to sing and praise the Lord in the beauty of holiness.

> *And when he had consulted with the people, he appointed those who should sing to the LORD, and who should praise the beauty of holiness, as they went out before the army and were saying:*

"Praise the LORD, For His mercy endures forever."

2 Chronicles 20:21

The Bible then tells us that when they began to sing and to praise, the Lord set ambushes against the people of Ammon, Moab, and Mount Seir, who had come against Judah, and they were defeated. The enemy destroyed one another and not one person from Judah was killed.

I believe that this is a picture of what happens when we praise our God *"in the beauty of holiness"*. Communication lines are destroyed and confusion breaks out in the enemy camp.

God also gave me some scriptures from the New Testament:

For though we walk in the flesh, we do not war according to the flesh. For the weapons of our warfare are not carnal but mighty in God for pulling down strongholds.

2 Corinthians 10:3-4

For we do not wrestle against flesh and blood, but against principalities, against powers, against the rulers of the darkness of this age, against spiritual hosts of wickedness in the heavenly places.

Ephesians 6:12

Today our battle is not against flesh and blood, but against principalities, against powers and the rulers of darkness. So, as in the Old Testament, God is sending out His musicians and singers ahead of the army, but this is a spiritual battle and there is a new sound, a new battle cry. This sound is an aggressive sound. It is also a prophetic sound that can be effective through any instrument including the voice. The very notes that the instruments play are speaking into situations bringing down strongholds.

I believe that praise and worship is a key to releasing the power of God and His Kingdom reign in a new and powerful way. I believe it is God's strategy for now, for the release of His power, for the church to rise up and advance and to defeat the power of darkness. God's desire is for us to rise up in powerful praise and intimate worship.

We have seen the levels of worship rise and a beautiful increase of His presence over the last few years, but there is so much more! We desire the fullness of His presence and when He comes, He comes with all His glory. It is in this atmosphere of "presence and glory" that His power is released in unprecedented ways; releasing salvation, healing, deliverance, revelation and breakthrough!

> *The Spirit of the LORD GOD is upon Me,*
> *Because the LORD has anointed Me*
> *To preach good tidings to the poor;*
> *He has sent Me to heal the broken-hearted,*
> *To proclaim liberty to the captives,*
> *And the opening of the prison to those who are*
> *bound;*
> *To give them beauty for ashes,*
> *The oil of joy for mourning,*
> *The garment of praise for the spirit of*
> *heaviness;*
> *That they may be called trees of righteousness,*
> *The planting of the Lord, that He may be*
> *glorified.*
>
> *Isaiah 61:1,3*

I could fill a whole book with testimonies of what God has done through the power of praise as we have travelled and ministered in different nations, towns and churches.

Wembley Christian Centre

Praise can bring breakthrough in difficult situations

In 1991 my dear friend Rev Soke Mun Ho and I were praying about where God wanted to take us next. So we gathered together with a couple of friends to worship and pray in tongues. We used to pray and worship for hours not even knowing what we were praying about! 'Suddenly' all became clear. Unknown to us, through praying in tongues, God had been preparing us for a new church plant in Wembley Park. It's a long story, however, by January 1992 we officially launched our new church, Wembley Christian Centre, under the umbrella of Kensington Temple. During the season leading up to this church plant God had been teaching me about prophetic warfare praise. We started our new church, with a small group, in a pub in Wembley Park in a function room called 'The Lord's Bar'.

The licensees of the pub loved us and even made us a sign saying 'Come on in and taste the new wine'! For six months we had a wonderful time in this pub and we actually led the licensees to the Lord! Our rent was only £20 a week including tea and coffee! A fantastic deal! Everything was going really well until our licensees left. New licensees arrived who hated us; they didn't want a church in their pub so they started inviting in a local psychic fair to operate in an adjacent hall.

One Sunday morning we were in The Lord's Bar and the psychic fair was next door in another function room. Well, we knew we were in a warfare situation and decided the best course of action was to extend our time of praise and to exalt

Jesus. So we did just that. We praised and worshipped Jesus and exalted Him. By the end of the morning the lady running the psychic fair came up to us and said that business was very slow that morning! Praise God! Because of our worship they were unable to operate. They never came back to the pub – we won the victory through the power of praise and worship.

Our landlords, however, were not happy about this and decided without any consultation with us, to put up our rent to £100 every week! So we asked God what to do. "Do we fight or do we look for another venue?" God told us to stay and fight. In fact He said to us, "This is your pub, you possess it!" "OK God, how do we do that?" we asked. "Through prophetic warfare praise," was His answer. The following Sunday I preached on the power of praise which was still a fresh revelation to me from heaven. We praised, exalted Jesus and pressed in until we felt the anointing to break through. That morning, as we worshipped, we knew we had possessed the pub in the spiritual realm.

All our battles are won firstly in the spiritual realm before they manifest in the natural realm.

After that Sunday we had no more problems with our landlords. We were able to negotiate with them a reasonable rent and we stayed in that pub for many years after that.

Dubai and Abu Dhabi

Praise releases miracles, healings, signs and wonders

For many years we had the privilege of ministering in Dubai and Abu Dhabi in the Arab Emirates. I used to love leading worship there because the people were so passionate and loved to worship.

One year we were invited to help lead a conference called *Freedom in Christ*. I was leading the worship accompanied by a wonderful local band. The people were so passionate, one morning they all (about 250) left their seats and gathered around me and the band and worshipped for about an hour and a half. During that time we only managed to sing two songs. We were just worshipping spontaneously and declaring God's goodness, love and faithfulness. After that the Pastor's wife got up and encouraged us to pray in tongues together for one hour!

The atmosphere was full of God's presence; there were many spontaneous healings and deliverances that morning because the praise and worship had released God's presence. No one even had to pray or touch anyone, God did it! In one meeting the pastor laid out a carpet, about twelve by six feet, at the front of the church and asked anyone who suffered with bronchitis to come up and step on the carpet. One by one they came up, stood on the carpet, and without anyone touching them, returned to their seat completely healed! God is so good.

Party in the Park – Pitstone – UK

Praise releases revelation and wisdom from heaven
Praise prepares hearts and breaks through for evangelism

My husband Brian and I live in a large village called Pitstone which is on the border of Hertfordshire, Bedfordshire and Buckinghamshire. For a season we were leading a house church in our home and also holding regular intercession and worship meetings in different venues in the area.

This area is known by some as 'the Valley of Praise'. It runs from Aylesbury down the A41 through Berkhamsted and Hemel Hempstead down to Watford. God had passed on a baton to us, concerning advancing His Kingdom in the valley through the power of praise, worship and intercession (*Harp and Bowl*, Revelation 5:8). We ran with this vision for a number of years, digging up wells and *"breaking up the fallow ground,"* (Hosea 10:12) along the valley, but especially in our own village of Pitstone.

> *And Isaac dug again the wells of water which they had dug in the days of Abraham his father, for the Philistines had stopped them up after the death of Abraham.*
>
> *Genesis 26:18*

Isaac dug up natural wells that the Philistines had blocked. However, we were unblocking spiritual wells; ancient wells of revivals, healings and past moves of God, to be restored again in our nation.

One morning, while we were worshipping and praising God and singing the scripture from Colossians 1:9 *"Fill us with the knowledge of your will"*, God gave me a vision of a large tent in Pitstone. I knew then that God wanted us to have an evangelistic crusade on Pitstone Green.

It was a massive vision. I felt that God wanted to provide a banquet of His love for the people of Pitstone. It took many years to fulfil this vision. We never let go of this vision, but continued to dig the well in Pitstone through our monthly *Harp and Bowl* worship and intercession meetings. This prepared the spiritual atmosphere for the event. To have such an event in a place as small as Pitstone we really needed God's timing and for Him to prepare the ground.

After many years the time arrived. The vision was too big for us and too expensive for us to run with on our own, we knew we needed the participation of other Christians in the village. There was no visible church in Pitstone at the time, but many

Christians lived in the village and travelled out to other towns to attend church. We gathered the few Christians that we knew locally and shared the vision. They enthusiastically embraced the idea and dipped into their pockets to finance the whole project. I believe because of the preparation and partnering with God in this vision it was a great success!

We had a three-day evangelistic mission on Pitstone Green called *Party on the Green*. Someone loaned us a stage and PA, and churches from the area sent in teams of musicians and singers. There was live music all day, for three days. In the evenings, our dear friend Rev Marilyn Harry preached the Gospel in her tent. Free BBQ (we gave away over 1500 hotdogs and hamburgers), drinks, cakes and refreshments were provided for all, plus bouncy castles and many other events for the children. There was prophetic evangelism and many people were encouraged with destiny words, a healing tent plus many other stalls. Just as God had said, everything was *free*.

All the Christians in the village and the region gathered around the vision and gave whatever they could. Some gave money, some gave food, some served on the stands, some served food and drink, some served the children, others provided overnight security and some provided tents. It was a very exciting time; there was such unity amongst the Christians and nobody wanted it to end.

Many people heard the Gospel for the first time; received healing, were saved, encouraged and received prophetic words. To this day the village has continued to run a similar secular event for charity on the village green every summer, but of course, now people have to pay for everything! Before our event, nothing like this had taken place on the village green, it was a breakthrough event for the village. Isn't God good!

Praise changes the spiritual atmosphere in cities, towns and regions

We recently had the privilege of ministering in Anglesey with the *Love Wales* team; a wonderful group of people led by Rev Marilyn Harry dedicated to bringing the Gospel to every village and town and region in Wales. We were invited to lead worship in Anglesey, for a special meeting that was held for all those who wanted to come and praise and intercede for the Island of Anglesey. We had a fantastic evening with many coming along from the island and even a team of prophetic dancers turned up out of the blue from Liverpool. We had a wild time of warfare praise, followed by strong intercession, encouraging prophetic words and inspiring prophetic dancing. It was a real team effort. The outcome was amazing; reports came in that something had shifted in the atmosphere over the island and we were asked would we come back for more!

Praise breaks chains and sets the captives free

There are many accounts in the Bible of God breaking into situations through the power of praise and worship. One such account is the story of Paul and Silas in Acts 16. They were bound and chained in prison but in the middle of the night, instead of having a pity party, they decided to have a praise party.

As they worshipped and praised the Lord, there was a great earthquake, the foundations of the prison were shaken and immediately all the doors were opened and everyone's chains were loosed. I think God was looking down from heaven and was so impressed by the music that He started to tap His feet and of course what followed was a mighty earthquake, that not only opened their chains and the prison doors, but also people's hearts to the Gospel. Thanksgiving and praise often opens the door to the miraculous.

The Voice of the Lord

The voice of the LORD is over the waters;
The God of glory thunders;
The LORD is over many waters.
The voice of the LORD is powerful;
The voice of the LORD is full of majesty.

Psalm 29:3-4

I am sure that many reading this book have received at some time a prophetic word. If you have, you will know what an encouragement it is.

Prophecy:

- Reveals the will and heart of God
- Unlocks destiny
- Imparts faith
- Releases healing, breakthrough and vision
- Releases the creative miracle working power of God
- Is affirming and encouraging

When there is a prophetic anointing on the music, God's voice is released in the same way, but through the power of music and sound. Sometimes when I play the piano, I know that I am playing a prophetic song. God speaks through the music imparting His will into a situation, bringing breakthrough, healing and His creative power. Quite often someone in the congregation will get up and bring the interpretation of the song.

Prophecy can come through many different ways. It can come through a spoken prophecy given to individuals, churches and even nations, but it can also come through singing, through instruments, through dance, through banners, through art (people painting pictures through the worship). We have such a creative God.

I love the sound of a shofar. It is the most aggressive instrument I have ever heard. What makes all this prophetic? It is the voice of God flowing through the people, the instruments, the dance, etc. His voice can move in very many ways to establish His will.

The Voice of God in Creation

> *And the Spirit of God was hovering over the face of the waters. Then God said, "Let there be light"; and there was light.*
>
> *Genesis 1:2b-3*

In Genesis 1 the Bible explains how God created the world. The Holy Spirit was hovering, and God spoke *"Let there be light, and there was light"*. In the same way the word of God also carries creative power in our mouths as we declare, decree, sing and prophesy.

The voice of God brings down walls of impossible situations

> *So the people shouted when the priests blew the trumpets. And it happened when the people heard the sound of the trumpet, and the people shouted with a great shout, that the wall fell down flat.*
>
> *Joshua 6:20*

How did the walls of Jericho fall down? I believe that it was the sound of God's voice through the shout of the people, the shofar, and their obedience to follow His instructions. There is no limit to what God can do through the sound of His voice.

Assyria was brought down by the power of His voice through the tambourine and harp

> *For through the voice of the Lord Assyria will be beaten down,*

As He strikes with the rod.
And in every place where the staff of punishment
passes,
Which the LORD lays on him,
It will be with tambourines and harps.

Isaiah 30:31-32

Who would have thought the harp and tambourines could be such warfare instruments? God can use any instrument which we give to Him to fulfil His purposes.

Let the warriors arise and let His voice flow through us to bring down the strongholds. Let us, (the church) arise as one man, one voice in unity. Together in God we are unstoppable!

2

Apostolic Governmental Warfare and Worship

Several years ago Kensington Temple, the church we attended in London, had a vision to plant hundreds of churches within the boundary of the M25 by the year 2000. We used to have the most amazing worship times during which we would enter right into the throne room of God. The worship was very grand; we all experienced the greatness and awesome presence of our God. At times the praise was so powerful that we would clap, stamp our feet and shout our praise to God with such zeal and joy for fifteen to twenty minutes. When the leaders came onto the stage to lead us onto the next part of the service, our praise ascended even higher and even more powerfully!

I remember thinking and wondering what impact this praise was having on London? At the time of this amazing worship, our church planting programme was very fruitful. We were planting a new church every week. I cannot prove it, but I am sure that the success of the church planting programme and the high praises rising up out of the central church were definitely connected.

I believe that the music ministry has an apostolic governmental role. We are called to change the atmosphere over cities and regions, to bring a shift in the spiritual realm and to advance the Kingdom of God on earth through the power of our praise and worship. We are called to move with heaven and to bring the sound of heaven to earth. We are called to prepare the way for the King of Kings to come in all His glory. When He comes, He comes in all His power, releasing revival, deliverance, salvation, healing and even His judgements on earth.

My husband, Brian, loves to tell the story of an incident that happened in East London in the early 1980s. His church, along with about a dozen other churches, held a joint evangelistic crusade in East London with the Dutch Evangelist Hans Koornstra. Many were saved and there were also some remarkable healings. Those churches, which included Church of England, Elim, Assemblies of God, United Reformed Church, Baptist and others continued to fellowship together and for a time gathered their congregations together once a month on a Sunday night to celebrate. They also conducted monthly united prayer meetings. At one such prayer meeting early in 1981, Brian remembers that such a peon of praise went up to God that night that they never actually uttered a prayer all evening. Brian was not leading the meeting, but at the close, he stood and announced that they had bound something significant in the heavens that night.

1980-81 was a dark time in the UK, there was much inner city deprivation, racial tension, and mass unemployment. That certainly applied to East London at that time.

Just after our united prayer meeting, in April right through to August, riots started breaking out in deprived areas of many big cities. Hansworth in Birmingham, Chapeltown in Manchester, Toxteth in Liverpool, Moss Side in Manchester and Brixton in London. Fear swept across East London as milk bottles started to disappear from people's front doors as they were being stock piled to make Molotov cocktails, and shops boarded up their windows in preparation for the rioting that was expected to come.

No rioting in East London ever took place that year, and Brian is convinced that it was because churches united together and proclaimed His Lordship in song over the area.

The Tribe of Judah

Judah, you are he whom your brothers shall praise;
Your hand shall be on the neck of your enemies;
Your father's children shall bow down before you.

Genesis 49:8

The name Judah means 'Praise'. Jesus was from the tribe of Judah. When the tribes marched to war, every tribe had to go in the order prescribed by God. God had a purpose for ordering the tribes according to their calling, gifting and characteristics.

In his book *A Time to Advance,* Chuck Pierce explains so clearly the calling of the Tribe of Judah.

> The tribe of Judah always marched out first. Their call was to rule, to lead in battle and to worship. Worship and Warfare always go together. If you are called to worship, you are also called to war. If you are called to war, you are also called to worship. Worship and Warfare cannot be separated.

> Governmental rulership goes with war. The most important duty for Judah was to follow the ark. The other tribes then had to follow Judah. The

first three tribes were Judah, Issachar (they knew the times and the seasons) and Zebulun (ability to prosper in business and trade). They would lead the nation to war against physical enemies. They also had the ability to overcome spiritually. Each of these tribes had a key in overturning Satan. Judah was called to worship.

In the original order of heaven, Lucifer was created to worship with pipes, strings and timbrels formed in his body.

> *You were in Eden, the garden of God;*
> *Every precious stone was your covering:*
> *The sardius, topaz, and diamond,*
> *Beryl, onyx, and jasper,*
> *Sapphire, turquoise, and emerald with gold.*
> *The workmanship of your timbrels and pipes*
> *Was prepared for you on the day you were*
> *created.*
>
> *Ezekiel 28:13*

He was heaven's worship leader, but he fell when he tried to exalt himself above God. Judah had a unique ability to overcome Satan.

Praise silences the enemy and the avenger.

> *O LORD, our Lord, how majestic is your name in all the earth! You have set your glory above the heaven. From the lips of children and infants you have ordained praise because of your enemies, to silence the foe and the avenger. (NIV) version*
>
> *Psalm 8:1-2*

The Governmental Role of Worship

> *Immediately I was in the Spirit; and behold, a throne set in heaven, and One sat on the throne... Before the throne there was a sea of glass, like crystal. And in the midst of the throne, and around the throne, were four living creatures full of eyes in front and in back.... And they do not rest day or night, saying:*

> *"Holy, holy, holy,*
> *Lord God Almighty,*
> *Who was and is and is to come!"*

> *...the twenty-four elders fall down before Him who sits on the throne and worship Him who lives forever and ever, and cast their crowns before the throne, saying:*

> *"You are worthy, O Lord,*
> *To receive glory and honour and power;*
> *For You created all things,*
> *And by Your will they exist and were created."*

> *Revelation 4:2-11*

This is a picture, in Revelation, of the throne of God. The throne of God is where the Government of the Universe takes place. The throne of God is surrounded by the continual worship of the four living creatures and the twenty-four elders, accompanied by the voices of ten thousand times ten thousand angels worshipping God.

> *And every creature which is in heaven and on the earth and under the earth and such as are in the sea, and all that are in them...*

> *Revelation 5:13*

As they worship around the throne, God responds to their worship.

Every time they declare God's will in worship there is a response.

For example, they declare in song:

> *"You are worthy to take the scroll, and to open its seals."*

Revelation 5:9

This declaration is followed by Jesus opening the scrolls.

More worship follows, after which the trumpet judgements are opened and then even more worship, which releases the opening of the bowls of judgement.

God always responds to our worship. There is power and authority in our worship to release the hand of God, His Government and His Kingdom on earth.

Three times in the Psalms (Psalm 96, 98 and 149) we are commanded to sing a 'new song' to the Lord and bless His name for all the things He has done for us. A new song is a fresh spontaneous expression of our thanks to God for who He is and what He has done.

Our new sound and our new song release the hand of God to fight on our behalf! Look at the scripture below; God is saying that as we sing a new song to Him we are releasing Him to go forth like a mighty man and fight for us!

> *Sing to the Lord a new song,*
> *And His praise from the ends of the earth...*
> *The Lord shall go forth like a mighty man;*
> *He shall stir up His zeal like a man of war.*
> *He shall cry out, yes, shout aloud;*

He shall prevail against His enemies.

Isaiah 42:10,13

When you are going into battle and the enemy has invaded you and is oppressing you, the Bible says to sound a blast of the trumpet before the Lord and God will pay attention. God took note of this sound of the trumpet and fought their battles.

> *When you go to war in your land against the enemy who oppresses you, then you shall sound an alarm with the trumpets, and you will be remembered before the Lord your God, and you will be saved from your enemies.*

Numbers 10:9

An example of this is found in *2 Chronicles 13-14;*

> *Jeroboam caused an ambush to go around behind them; so they were in front of Judah, and the ambush was behind them. And when Judah looked around, to their surprise the battle line was at both front and rear; and they cried out to the Lord, and the priests sounded the trumpets.*

There was a war between Jeroboam, King of Israel, and Abijah, King of Judah. Jeroboam was the aggressor in this situation. Abijah called on God declaring that he had right on his side, a divine right:

> *"You know, or ought to know, that God gave the kingdom to David and his sons for ever."*

2 Chronicles 13:5

He knew God was with Him and called on Him for help. They found themselves ambushed by Jeroboam's armies both behind them and in front of them. So Abijah and Judah cried out to the Lord and the priests sounded the trumpets. Immediately God responded and wiped out their enemies. They had called on the Lord and they were triumphant!

> *God struck Jeroboam and all Israel before Abijah and Judah. And the children of Israel fled before Judah, and God delivered them into their hand.*
>
> *2 Chronicles 13:15-17*

Ecclesia

The word 'church' occurs more than one hundred times in the New Testament. Today many people connect the word 'church' to a building. This was not the case in New Testament times.

If the original text 'church' was meant to relate to a building, the word used would have been *'kuriakon'*, literally meaning the building which belongs to the Lord or the Lord's House.

However, the Greek word used in the New Testament one hundred and fifteen times is not' *'kuriakon'* but *'ecclesia'* which has nothing to do with buildings.

'Ecclesia' means governmental assembly, the called out ones, the elected body who were called to rule and make decisions concerning the culture and the values of the city over which they rule. They were 'the gatekeepers' who decided what was or was not allowed to come through the gates.

Jesus says we, the church, are His *'ecclesia'*, called out by God to be His gatekeepers, to change the values and the culture of the world around us.

*"And I also say to you that you are Peter, and on this rock I will build my **ecclesia,** and the gates of Hades shall not prevail against it And I will give you the keys of the kingdom of heaven, and whatever you bind on earth will be bound in heaven, and whatever you loose on earth will be loosed in heaven. "*

Matthew 16:18-19

In the same way, when we release our praise and our worship to God we release His hand of power and victory over our lives, cities and nations.

God is calling us to rule and reign with Him.

The Warrior Bride

3

The God of Glory Thunders

The Lord thundered from heaven,
And the Most High uttered His voice,
Hailstones and coals of fire.

Psalm 18:13

There is a new sound for every new season. There is power in the sound of heaven to bring breakthrough.

> *After it a voice roars;*
> *He thunders with His majestic voice,*
> *And He does not restrain them when His voice*
> *is heard.*
> *God thunders marvellously with His voice;*
> *He does great things which we cannot*
> *comprehend.*
> *For He says to the snow, 'Fall on the earth';*
> *Likewise to the gentle rain and the heavy rain*
> *of His strength.*

Job 37:4-6

God is taking us to new levels in praise and worship

There is spiritual power in sound. Power to change the environment and power to change the season. Each season is determined and defined by a new sound.

The new sound breaks the old cycle.

In Creation God spoke:

> *Then God said, "Let there be light"; and there was light.*

> *Genesis 1:3*

When Jesus was born there was a new sound, as hosts of angels appeared, and the skies were filled with the sounds of praise.

> *And suddenly there was with the angel a multitude of the heavenly host praising God and saying: "Glory to God in the highest, and on earth peace, goodwill toward men!"*

> *Luke 2:13-14*

In the Acts of the Apostles, on the Day of Pentecost, tongues and flames of fire descended on the heads of the apostles. The very first thing they experienced was the sound of a violent wind from heaven:

> *When the Day of Pentecost had fully come, they were all with one accord in one place. And suddenly there came a sound from heaven, as of a rushing mighty wind, and it filled the whole house where they were sitting. Then there appeared to them divided tongues, as of fire, and one sat upon each of them. And they were all filled with the Holy Spirit and began to speak with other tongues as the Spirit gave them utterance.*

> *Acts 2:1-4*

Sound is important to God and is very powerful. The universe of God is full of sound. Creation itself is full of sound:

> *All the trees of the field shall clap their hands.*

> *Isaiah 55:12*

The physical heavens continually declare sound:

> *While the morning stars sang together and all the angels shouted for joy?*

> *Job 38:7*

Sound cannot travel through space, and so we can never hear the stars. However, scientists, using a technique called asteroseismology, are able to detect the flickers of light coming from some stars and reconstruct the sound produced by the stars. Some stars evidently vibrate like a musical instrument that can be translated into a harmonic hum.

What is sound? The science of sound

Sound is vibration and it travels through matter in the form of waves. It can be heard and be seen. Bats can fly at high speed seeing by sound. There is a lot more to sound than we understand.

An army does not march in step over a bridge, as the vibration of the marching may cause the bridge to collapse, similar to when a singer hits a certain sound and breaks the glass.

> When an army marches across a bridge, the soldiers often "break step" so that their rhythmic marching will not start resonating throughout the bridge. A sufficiently large army marching at just the right cadence could set the deadly vibration into motion.

> *How Science Works*

In a similar way the footfall of the pedestrians on the new Millennium Bridge in London caused a vibration that necessitated the closure of the bridge for modifications shortly after it was opened in June 2000.

What does sound look like?

A 16th century German scientist discovered how to see sound. If you bombard a metal plate that has sand on it with sound, the sounds form patterns. Every note has a different shape! The sound was imprinting itself on the sand.

When the God of glory thunders His voice, He releases His spiritual power and sets us free.

> *The voice of the LORD is over the waters;*
> *The God of glory thunders;*
> *The LORD is over many waters.*
> *The voice of the LORD is powerful;*
> *The voice of the LORD is full of majesty.*
> *The voice of the LORD breaks the cedars,*
> *Yes, the LORD splinters the cedars of Lebanon.*
> *....The voice of the LORD divides the flames of fire.*
> *The voice of the LORD shakes the wilderness;*
> *...The voice of the LORD makes the deer give birth,*
> *And strips the forests bare.*
>
> *Psalm 29:3-9*

Every revival has its own sound. To name a few: the Jesus movement of the 1960s and 70s had its own sound; the Toronto Outpouring of the Father's love had a sound; the Pensacola Revival had a sound. You may remember the song *Mercy Seat* sung by a teenage girl, every time you heard it, you wanted to get saved again!

Every revival in history brought a new sound to break the church out of bondage. The Wesleyan Revival brought a new sound with the hymns of Charles Wesley. The Reformation brought a new sound of singing. Martin Luther wrote, "Next to the Word of God, music deserves the highest praise," and Luther himself wrote many hymns.

The Bible encourages us to praise loudly

It terrifies the enemy!

Here are some of the different Hebrew words used in the Old Testament for 'praise', describing different kinds of sound:

Ruah: (literally means) to split the ear with sound. It usually means shouting loudly or blowing a loud trumpet blast. Shouting often took place just before a people or army rushed into battle against opposition. Sometimes the war cry became the very signal used to commence engagement with the enemy.

Teruah: also to split the ear with sound; to praise God loudly.

A shout of alarm, a battle cry. It refers to a loud, sharp shout or cry in general, but it often indicates a shout of joy or victory.

Some people complain about loud noise in a church service and explain 'God is not deaf'! But we need to remember, He is not nervous either!

Halal: (forms the word Hallelujah) means to praise God in unrestrained celebration, to have a loud, joyful celebration or party for the Lord.

In a *Halal* all sorts of loud musical instruments were used to increase the intensity of praise to God (Psalm 150).

Have a *Halal* for Yahweh. Have a celebration for the Lord.

A Jewish Rabbi describes the ***'Halal'*** as:

> 'To shine; a brilliant, radiant, conspicuous shine that can't be ignored,
>
> Make a show of celebrating with boasting and continuous, noisy, foolish-sounding raving'.

> *Praise (**Halal**) Him with the sound of the trumpet;*
> *Praise (**Halal**) Him with the lute and harp!*
> *Praise (**Halal**) Him with the timbrel and dance;*
> *Praise (**Halal**) Him with stringed instruments and flutes!*
> *Praise (**Halal**) Him with loud cymbals;*
> *Praise (**Halal**) Him with clashing cymbals*
> *Let everything that has breath praise (**Halal**) the Lord.*
> *Praise (**Halal**) the Lord.*
>
> *Psalm 150:3-5*

Tehillah: means to sing praises: a song of praise.

> *God is enthroned on the (**Tehillah**) of His people.*
>
> *Psalm 22:3*

Zamar: to praise God on an instrument, sing praises with musical accompaniments. Pluck the strings and drum with the fingers.

Yadah: physically, to throw a stone, an arrow, especially to revere or worship with extended hands.

> *"Praise (**Yadah**) the Lord,*
> *For His mercy endures forever."*
>
> *2 Chronicles 20:21*

Ruah and Teruah were the key in bringing in God's presence:

> *Thus all Israel brought up the ark of the covenant of the Lord with shouting (**Teruah**) and with the sound of the horn, with trumpets and with cymbals, making music with stringed instruments and harps.*

> *1 Chronicles 15:28*

> *As the Ark of the LORD came into the camp, all Israel shouted (**Ruah**) with a great shout (**Teruah**) so that the earth resounded.*
> *When the Philistines heard the noise of (**Teruah**), They said, "What does the noise of this great (**Teruah**) in the camp of the Hebrews mean?" Then they understood that the Ark of the LORD had come into the camp.*
> *The Philistines were afraid, for they said,*
> *"GOD HAS COME INTO THE CAMP! Woe to us!*
> *For nothing like this has happened before!"*

> *1 Samuel 4:5-7*

How amazing that when we release our praise to God, the enemy is terrified! Praise God we need to do that more often.

Tsarach: A verb indicating a roar, war cry. It refers to the Lord's utterance of a war cry of attack as He goes forth to battle.

This scripture teaches us that as we release our praise to God we are releasing Him to fight on our behalf! Our God is a mighty man of war, He is a warrior God!

> *Sing to the Lord a new song,*
> *And His praise from the ends of the earth...*

The Lord shall go forth like a mighty man;

He shall stir up His zeal like a man of war.

*He shall cry out (**Tsarach**), yes, shout aloud (**Tsarach**);*

He shall prevail against His enemies.

Isaiah 42:10, 13

The quiet sedate worship found in many English churches is fine, but can hardly be described as warfare and doing battle in the heavenlies. The Hebrew words for praise and worship express something far more exuberant. Perhaps we need to get more excited about our God and release our battle cry and exuberant praise more often. We have so much to thank God for and to celebrate. I am sure if we did we would see much more breakthrough in our lives.

Shout of faith

The shout of faith is like an atomic bomb going off in the spiritual realm. When the people of God release a shout of faith, the atmosphere is shifted, and victory is released.

Jericho is a great example of the shout of faith. Those walls were impenetrable, but God gave the people of Israel a strategy to circle the city seven times for six days. On the seventh day they were to march around the city seven times and release the sound of the shofar and a shout of faith. They released the sound of breakthrough and victory!

> *It shall come to pass, when they make a long blast with the ram's horn, and when you hear the sound of the trumpet, that all the people shall shout with a great shout; then the wall of the city will fall down flat.*
>
> *Joshua 6:5*

4

Intimate Worship

I am my beloved's,
And my beloved is mine.

Song of Songs 6:3

The book of the *Song of Songs* was written by Solomon to his beloved bride, but also it is the 'Song of all Songs' written by Jesus, the greatest lover in the universe, to us, His beloved Bride, the Church.

We are all the Body of Christ and we are all the beautiful Bride that Jesus gave His life for. This is the song of Jesus and the song of the Holy Spirit to us His Bride. He is loving us, wooing us and romancing us into maturity. He is calling us into a greater depth of love, romance and revelation than ever before.

> *O my dove, in the clefts of the rock,*
> *In the secret places of the cliff,*
> *Let me see your face,*
> *Let me hear your voice;*
> *For your voice is sweet,*
> *And your face is lovely.*

Song of Songs 2:14

There is a limit on how long we can serve someone through gritted teeth and sheer determination. However, when we love someone passionately there is no limit to what we will do, or the lengths we will go to follow them and please them. As Heidi Baker of *Iris Ministries* says, we are "laid down lovers". We will go where He goes, say what He says, pray what He prays, and do what He does.

Jesus is wooing His Bride into greater depth and love than ever before. He is pouring out His Spirit in a greater way than ever before, wooing us into His presence. Yes, the battle is heating up and intensifying but He is pouring out His presence increasingly on His church. In His presence there is peace and joy. He wants us to know who we are in Him, so we fight from a place of peace, joy and security.

The Bride of Christ – a Bridal Paradigm

All who are redeemed by the blood of the Lamb are the Bride of Christ! Sorry guys, you are the Bride of Christ; however, we ladies are also the sons of God!

God is preparing His Bride for the Marriage Supper of the Lamb.

> *Let us be glad and rejoice and give Him glory,*
> *for the marriage of the Lamb has come, and His*
> *wife has made herself ready.*

> *Revelation 19:7*

I am sure most of us have been to a wedding, either our own or of someone else. How did the bride look? Was she radiant or did she look tired and worn out? Most brides I have seen on their wedding day are radiant and beautiful. However, the Body of Christ is often tired, worn out and beaten down. God is preparing a beautiful, triumphant, radiant bride for His Son.

We are definitely a work in progress!

When you were walking down the aisle or waiting by the altar for your beloved, (if you have been married) what were you thinking about? Were you thinking about the wedding breakfast? Were you worrying about whether the chauffeur knew the way from the venue to the reception? No, of course not. I am sure you were excitedly and passionately gazing on the face of your beloved and looking forward, with great anticipation, to your lives together.

> *...that He might present her to Himself a glorious church, not having spot or wrinkle or any such thing, but that she should be holy and without blemish.*
>
> *Ephesians 5:27*

In the same way God is preparing us, a vibrant, spotless and passionate bride for His Son Jesus. That's why He died; to bring us to a place of maturity to be His counterpart.

Quote from *Divine Romance* by Gene Edwards

> Life pulsated, light blazed in newfound glory. Love ascended. The very being of God shook in the apprehending of this revelation. And what was that revelation? That there could be two! ...An all-knowing God had brought forth a thought so exciting that even He trembled in its afterglow. Then exulting in revelation, He consecrated His whole being to this one task: to have ...a bride.

The Song of Songs

> *Let Him kiss me with kisses of his mouth*
> *For Your love is better than wine,*
> *Because of the fragrance of your good ointments,*

The Warrior Bride

Your name is ointment poured forth,
Draw me away and we will run after you
The King has brought me into His chambers
We will be glad and rejoice in You.

Song of Songs 1:2-4

The Song of Songs has transformed my life. The bride experiences the exhilaration of being kissed by Jesus. You can interchange the word 'mouth' with 'word'. When God touches us, He brings transformation. The cry of her heart is; 'touch me and transform me.' To her, His love is better than any earthly pleasures; even better than the exhilaration of wine. When we are being embraced by His love there is no other pleasure that is superior. That is the cry of her heart and mine; draw us into your heart and let us experience your love in a greater way. God is the only one who knows us intimately and knows how to access our heart to bring healing and the knowledge of His perfect love.

His Name is ointment poured forth

He has been poured out for us in His death and resurrection. His fragrance is like none other. He is more lovely and beautiful than anything else. His name is so powerful yet so beautiful. Like a rose that has been crushed, he has been crushed for us and His fragrance is poured out over us and through our lives.

> *Now thanks be to God who always leads us in triumph in Christ, and through us diffuses the fragrance of His knowledge in every place. For we are to God the fragrance of Christ among those who are being saved and among those who are perishing. To the one we are the aroma of death leading to death, and to the other the aroma of life leading to life.*

2 Corinthians 2:14-16

Draw me away and we will run after you

This is the Bride's heart cry for intimacy and partnership with Jesus. We can't have one without the other. If we run without Jesus, without an intimate love relationship, we will burn out. We need to sustain the balance of our time alone with Him in the secret place and our service in the world and to the Body of Christ.

The King has brought me into his chambers

This speaks of encounters with Jesus and those moments, when God steps into our lives and supernaturally draws us away. In these moments He speaks words of destiny into our hearts that changes us forever.

Oh God! Let us have more of those life-changing moments. Let us draw near to Him, longing for more heart encounters with Him, learning to listen to the whisper of His Spirit into our spirit as we follow Him. This is the season for a greater presence and awareness of the Holy Spirt; following Him, listening to Him, aligning with Him. He knows what we need to do and where we need to go.

The Warrior Bride

5

Our Roots: King David and the Tabernacle

Moreover David and the captains of the army separated for the service some of the sons of Asaph, of Heman, and of Jeduthun, who should prophesy with harps, stringed instruments, and cymbals.

1 Chronicles 25:1

In order to be effective in our ministry we need to know who we are and the great heritage that we have as God's music ministers.

When we understand our roots and our identity as music ministers, it gives us more understanding and authority when we minister. It is not just a few songs that we are singing on a Sunday morning to make us feel good, but God's rich calling on our lives to advance His rule and reign on earth through our praise and worship. Our calling is to lead the congregation in offering up spiritual sacrifices of worship to Him.

Our model for music ministry today is based on the revelation given to King David in the Tabernacle in Zion. For many years I couldn't understand how the music ministry pattern based in the Old Testament could be effective in a New Testament context until one day I heard some teaching on how David's revelation went through the cross because he was a type of New Testament believer.

David had an unusual relationship with God. He could go into the Tabernacle and sit in His presence before the Ark and not die! God gave him extraordinary grace and revelation.

> *Then King David went in and sat before the Lord.*

> *2 Samuel 7:18*

Prior to David and later in Solomon's time onward, only the High Priest could enter the Holy of Holies and set his eyes on the Ark of the Covenant and then just once per year with fear and trembling.

The restoration of true worship

> *After this I will return*
> *And will rebuild the tabernacle of David, which*
> *has fallen down;*
> *I will rebuild its ruins,*
> *And I will set it up.*

> *Acts 15:16*

I believe the worship services in David's day must have been awesome. In his day there were two tabernacles: one in Zion and one in Gibeon. The Ark of God was placed in the Tabernacle in Zion and the sacrifices and rituals took place in the Tabernacle in Gibeon. I think I would have preferred to be in Zion where all the worship took place.

Chenaniah was David's music director, appointed to lead all the worship leaders and teams.

> *Chenaniah, leader of the Levites, was instructor*
> *in charge of the music, because he was skilful.*

> *1 Chronicles 15:22*

David had three worship leaders: Asaph, Heman and Jeduthan. Each leader trained and discipled others. In total they were responsible for approximately 4000 singers and musicians. Groups were then formed from this body of musicians and singers who would minister to the Lord in song in the Tabernacle at Zion twenty-four hours a day, day and night.

> *A fire shall always be burning on the altar; it shall never go out.*

> *Leviticus 6:13*

Worship must have been awesome in those days with so many worshipping and prophesying with their voices and their instruments. They would have gone into the Tabernacle in Zion and come before the presence of the Lord. There they would have sung antiphonal songs and Psalms; singing and responding to one another in Psalms and hymns and spiritual songs.

However, I believe that God is not only restoring our prophetic anointing in the music ministry, but is also taking us far higher and deeper than ever before.

The Prophetic Mantle is our Inheritance

I love the prophetic in worship. I love to hear the drums or tambourine or piano played prophetically or see someone dancing prophetically. How exciting when a prophetic melody is played out on the keyboard then someone in the congregation receives the interpretation of what God is saying through the music.

I have experienced so many instances of God speaking through the music. After a time of prophetic worship, if we stop to ask what people have received from the Lord, there will always be some who have received encouraging words, pictures, visions etc that are appropriate to share with the congregation. Recently, while celebrating on New Year's Eve in our church, my friend played a beautiful solo on the cello, and while she was playing, the prophetic word was going forth of what God was saying, through the sound of the cello.

The prophetic anointing was on the music ministry from the very beginning in David's day and it is who we are; it is our inheritance. Today God is restoring the prophetic anointing on the music ministry.

> *The sons of Asaph were under the direction of Asaph, who prophesied according to the order of the king...The sons of Jeduthun under the direction of their father Jeduthun, who prophesied with a harp to give thanks and to praise the Lord...The sons of Heman, the king's seer in the words of God, to exalt his horn.*
>
> *1 Chronicles 25:2-5*

David's worship leaders regularly prophesied with their voices and their instruments. It was in fact an order of the King!

Let's stir it up!

As we stir up the prophetic in our hearts and in the congregation, then God will manifest his presence with even more intensity. Songs are the springboard for spontaneous and prophetic worship. As we seek to flow in the prophetic more and more, we release God's heart, passion, life and the 'now' word in season, through the power of praise and worship.

There are no limits to what God can do with us if we are willing to flow with Him into new heights and depths.

This is my challenge to you.

Are you willing to explore new heights and depths of worship and to jump out of the boat of safe songs, to soar into the realm of the Spirit through spontaneous and prophetic worship and bring the sounds of heaven to earth? I believe that when we do, nothing can stop the Kingdom of heaven advancing on earth and releasing His power in unprecedented ways. Let it be on earth as it is in Heaven.

The Warrior Bride

6

What is the Music Ministry?
Our Calling

Moreover David and the captains of the army separated for the service some of the sons of Asaph, of Heman, and of Jeduthun, who should prophesy with harps, stringed instruments, and cymbals.

1 Chronicles 25:1

Music ministry is a high calling from God and God requires excellence. Our calling and anointing comes from God and our recognition comes from man. We can't just one day decide, "Oh, I think I'll join the music team", like one would say, "Oh, I think I'll have a nice cup of tea!" We need to know that this is where God wants us. It is a high calling that demands excellence, commitment and a lifestyle of purity and holiness that backs up our calling.

How do we know we are called to the music ministry? I believe it begins with our passion. We love to worship; we are worshippers at home as well as in church. We have skill and abilities and talents in this area too. I remember as a young Christian watching a music minister bringing a prophetic song to the church one Sunday morning and thinking, 'this is what I want to do, this is what I want to bring to the church.' Something in my heart rose up that morning with a big 'YES' Lord!

I knew I was called into the music ministry. When I was born again back in the 80s God gave me a dream where He clearly showed me that my ministry was on the keyboard and singing. From that time on I have been on adventure after adventure with God. I always look to increase the boundaries of my experience of Him because I have discovered that my worship comes out of my revelation of Him and His glory. If I become stagnant in my worship, the remedy is not finding a new song or trying a new technique, but the remedy is always seeking His Face for new and fresh encounters with Him.

In the music ministry there are four main points of focus.

- Firstly, our key focus is to minister to the Lord, to flow with the Holy Spirit and release the sound of heaven.
- Secondly, our focus is to connect with the people we are leading and to take them on a journey.
- Thirdly, but equally important, is to be aware of and flow with, the singers and musicians who minister with us in order to travel together in unity.
- Our fourth focus, is playing our own instrument.

All this requires practice, trust and good communication skills. We are spinning four plates at once! The worship sets the scene in our services. When we lead worship at the beginning of the service we are rolling out the red carpet for our King of Glory to come and establish His Kingdom. It is as important as the preaching of the word. We are seen as leaders by the church, therefore we should conduct ourselves with grace, humility and purity. Our lives need to reflect our calling. The devil hates worshippers and especially worship leaders.

Remember he too was a worship leader and he was kicked out of heaven because of pride, as he sought to be equal to God.

God will test the motivation of our hearts again and again. To ascend the heights of worship that He desires for us and for the church: sin, pride and self-motivation must be nailed to the cross! We must keep our hearts right before Him, be quick to repent, and to preserve the unity of the Spirit in our teams and churches. Psalm133 declares that the anointing comes through unity.

> *Behold, how good and how pleasant it is*
> *For brethren to dwell together in unity!*
> *It is like the precious oil upon the head,*
> *...For there the Lord commanded the blessing*
> *Life forevermore.*
>
> *Psalm 133*

God wants His music ministers healed and whole, walking in the light and purity, so that we can receive everything He wants to give us. The ministry of worship is an important key in these last days, because we usher in the presence of our King. When the King comes in all His glory, people are healed, delivered, set free and saved. Churches, regions and nations can experience breakthrough power and shifting of atmospheres through the power of praise.

The Warrior Bride

7

Requirements of Music Ministers

Then one of the servants answered and said,
"Look, I have seen a son of Jesse the Bethlehemite, who is
skilful in playing, a mighty man of valour, a man of war,
prudent in speech, and a handsome person; and the Lord is
with him."

1 Samuel 16:18

This is a wonderful scripture about what God is looking for in His music ministers. It sums up perfectly what is needed. This verse, of course, is about David when he was first brought into the courts of Saul as the king's prophetic musician.

The qualities that God requires are: skill, anointing, character and an ability to communicate and minister to the people

1. Skill

So the number of them, with their brethren who were instructed in the songs of the Lord, all who were skilful, was two hundred and eighty-eight.

1 Chronicles 25:7

The first thing to look for when recruiting new members into the music team, is skill.

I would always recommend auditioning anyone who wants to join the team. Sometimes you might feel that the person has anointing, but needs to improve skill, if that is the case, you can recommend lessons for them. I was completely unable to play by ear and play spontaneously as my training had been focussed in classical piano.

To help me on my journey, I went to conferences and lessons. I received much prayer, I fasted and I practised and practised. Slowly I began to break out and God started to give me my own style of playing. Always audition singers with an instrument. I have had many experiences with singers who can sing very well on their own, but put them next to a piano or another singer, and you realise they are completely out of tune and unable to keep a tune. Maybe their calling is to be a solo singer! Never worry about not receiving someone into the ministry if you feel they are not good enough, because if you do receive them, they will not be happy and fulfilled and neither will the congregation. Perhaps their calling is doing something else where they would find greater fulfilment.

2. *Anointing*

If someone has the skill then the next thing to look for is the anointing. This is the most important thing in the music ministry. We can always improve our skill with lessons and practice, but without the anointing we just make a noise!

The anointing is the 'unction to function'. It is the gift of His presence when we are ministering. We simply can't minister without it. As music ministers we must know how to seek it, preserve it and flow in partnership with the Holy Spirit.

Our anointing reflects our walk with Jesus. As music ministers we need to take time to pray and wait on the Lord.

We need to take time in the Word of God, both reading and meditating on it, as the Word is our springboard into the prophetic. God can only use what is within us, hence the importance of knowing scripture. Also, we can be more confident that we are theologically correct when we sing the word.

The Bible does teach us that the gifts are given without repentance. However, the depth and level of the anointing reflects our walk with Him. Therefore, the anointing is linked very closely with our lifestyle and our character.

Listed here below are some of the fruit of the anointing:

- **The anointing breaks the heavy yoke**

  It shall come to pass in that day
  That his burden will be taken away from your
  shoulder,
  And his yoke from your neck,
  And the yoke will be destroyed because of the
  anointing oil.

  Isaiah 10:27

- **The anointing releases the prophetic word**

  "But now bring me a musician." Then it
  happened, when the musician played, that the
  hand of the LORD came upon him.

  2 Kings 3:15

Elisha in this scripture asked for a musician because the anointing on the musicians would release the prophetic word.

- **The anointing brings God's fragrance**

  Thus says David the son of Jesse;

Thus says the man raised up on high,
The anointed of the God of Jacob,
And the sweet Psalmist of Israel…

2 Samuel 23:1

Heaven has a fragrance. When we worship, God's fragrance is released into our lives and then we carry that fragrance with us wherever we go.

- **The anointing releases new songs**

Sing to Him a new song;
Play skilfully with a shout of joy.

Psalm 33:3

The anointing releases new songs. Whenever God pours out His Spirit, new spontaneous songs are released, bringing His 'now' word to the congregation.

- **The anointing brings the presence of the Lord –the Shekinah glory**

…indeed it came to pass, when the trumpeters and singers were as one, to make one sound to be heard in praising and thanking the Lord, and when they lifted up their voice with the trumpets and cymbals and instruments of music, and praised the Lord, … the house of the Lord, was filled with a cloud, so that the priests could not continue ministering because of the cloud; for the glory of the Lord filled the house of God.

2 Chronicles 5:13-14

This is what we long for, His glory poured out onto the people. We want Him to come and take control and touch His people.

3. Lifestyle and Character

> *Therefore, I urge you, brothers, in view of God's mercy, to offer your bodies as living sacrifices, holy and pleasing to God – this is your spiritual act of worship. (NIV)*

Romans 12:1

Our whole lives need to be a sacrifice of praise. Wherever we are in our individual walk with God will come out of us when we minister. Are we pursuing a life of holiness? Are there issues in our lives that are contrary to the Word of God that we are not correcting?

Is praise a way of life with us? Do we worship God at home? As music ministers we can't take people further than we go ourselves. We can't expect to be out on Saturday nights drinking and partying and then ministering and flowing in the anointing the following morning!

Does our lifestyle back up our confession or are we Sunday Christians who smile, worship, decree and declare on Sunday (or whenever we are leading worship) and then live a life contrary to God's best for the rest of the week? Are we walking the walk of faith or just talking the talk? We will never arise to the fullness of our calling if that is our approach. Remember we are set apart by God for this high and holy calling. Our lifestyle needs to reflect who we are and what God has called us to be.

If there are unresolved sins and issues in our lives we are open to attack from the enemy. When that is the case, God will protect us by not releasing us to operate in the highest levels until we are ready. Our lifestyle and character are more important to God than anything else, he does not want us targeted and destroyed by the enemy.

What are some of the key character requirements?

- **Humility**

  So Samuel said, "When you were little in your own eyes, were you not head of the tribes of Israel? And did not the Lord anoint you king over Israel?"

  1 Samuel 15:17

Remember Satan was chief worship leader in heaven and was thrown out of heaven because of pride; he wanted to be equal with God.

The anointing comes when we are humble. *"God resists the proud, but gives grace to the humble," James 4:6.* We don't need 'prima donnas' in the music ministry. Our part is to serve the local church with humility and submission to God and to the Pastor.

- **Purity of heart**

What is your motive for being in the music ministry?

  ...be an example to the believers in word, in conduct, in love, in spirit, in faith, in purity.

  1 Timothy 4:12

Do we love being up the front? Is our ministry bringing glory to Jesus or to ourselves? We must be sure we have a pure motive and to hold the ministry very lightly. Never hold the ministry tightly, but always be ready to lay it down again and again. If we don't, God will take it from us. Otherwise it becomes an idol before God and He is a jealous God.

One way to find out our motivation is how we feel after having spent precious time preparing the worship and then the pastor decides to do something different from what we had planned. How we feel then, signifies whether we are performers or true worshippers!

- **Faithfulness**

  And the things that you have heard from me among many witnesses, commit these to faithful men who will be able to teach others also.

  2 Timothy 2:2

I used to know someone years ago who was exceptionally talented and anointed, however this person constantly let himself down by his inconsistency and unreliability. God requires faithfulness; there is no limit to what God can do with a faithful person.

When I pastored in Wembley I used to receive calls from members of the band telling me that they'd had a bad week and were too tired to come and minister and would I release them? Or sometimes they just wouldn't turn up to minister at all. And then there was music practice! My old Pastor used to say the only reason we don't turn up for a music practice is if we have a death certificate! Remember, the devil hates us and he laughs when we turn over and go to sleep, or when we let some bad experience stop us going forward. There have been many times when I have felt as spiritual as a cabbage and wanted to drop through the floor. But as my husband always says to me 'stand in the grace of God'. I just come before God, ask for His cleansing and His empowering and step out by faith. Sometimes those times are the most powerful times of ministry, because I am so dependent on Him and aware of my own inadequacies.

Do we know this is our calling? Have we made a quality decision to serve God in the music ministry? Is it on His terms or ours? Will we commit to go to music practice even when it's blowing a blizzard and we don't feel like it? Will we commit to turn up and minister whatever is going on and when it is the last thing in the world we want to do? Are we going to stick with it even when things are not easy? These are important questions and God will test our hearts to see how serious we are, because He wants a partnership with us that He can trust.

4. Ministry and ability to communicate

The worship leader must bridge the gap between the musicians and the hearers. This area must be developed as much as skill and anointing.

When I first began leading worship in my own church at Wembley I used to shut my eyes tightly and off I went hoping that everybody would follow me. I didn't like to see the faces of the people looking at me, so I kept my eyes tight shut for the duration of our worship time.

On one occasion my friend, Soke Mun, said to me, "One day you will open your eyes and everybody will have left!" Well that really convicted me and I determined that day to work on my communication skills with the congregation. There are different types of worship leader (outlined in a separate chapter) and some find it easier than others. My preferred style of leading was to simply lead by worshipping myself, but without much interaction with the congregation. I soon realised that I had to make a connection with the congregation if I was going to lead anyone anywhere!

- **They presented themselves in fine linen**

  David was clothed with a robe of fine linen, as were all the Levites who bore the ark, the singers, and Chenaniah the music master with the singers.

  1 Chronicles 15:27

70

Do we look good? Are people inspired when they look at us? People need to look at us and be inspired to worship. It's important, too, not to wear clothes that distract people from Jesus. Don't dress to kill! On the other hand, we need to look presentable. Also, do we look like Jesus has done something for us when we worship, or do we look as though we have drunk a glass of vinegar? I always remember a lady in Kensington Temple who, when she worshipped, lit up the platform with her countenance; her love for Jesus was very real. It was infectious and an inspiration.

We used to minister a lot in the far south of Chile. Brian, my husband, would preach and I would lead worship on my piano. My piano would travel everywhere with us! At some of the services, some of the pretty young girls would get up on the platform and play their ukuleles, and they would look so serious, yet when they got off the platform their beautiful smiles would light up their faces. For some reason they thought it was not right to smile whilst ministering. Maybe they thought that they did not look holy if they looked happy! Let's ensure that our faces reflect our joy and delight in Him!

Godly leadership and order

> *All these were under the direction of their father for the music in the house of the LORD, with cymbals, stringed instruments, and harps, for the service of the house of God. Asaph, Jeduthun, and Heman were under the authority of the king.*

1 Chronicles 25:6

There was proper order and levels of submission. Asaph, Heman and Jeduthun were responsible for the growth and development of those under them. They also were in submission to the king, which for us today would be the pastor or the leader of the church.

It is very important to be aware of God's order in the church. The pastor is similar to the king. The worship leader is always under the authority of the pastor. When the worship leader leads the church he carries full authority which has been given to him by the pastor. But when the pastor comes on the platform and wants to take over, even if the worship leader disagrees with him and his timing etc., the worship leader must always step aside and give way to the pastor. In a similar way when the worship leader leads, the band and singers give their full support, even if they don't like the choice of songs or direction. Unity and God's order is very important in the kingdom.

I have also learnt that God gives direction and the blueprint to the leader so that they can lead. Even though we do not agree sometimes with the direction taken by our leaders, we need to remember that they have the blueprint, the bigger picture and the final accountability to God.

Many years ago I had the privilege of co-leading the women's ministry in Kensington Temple. We hosted a three-day ladies conference. It was a huge event and I was asked to organise the worship for it. We had a large band plus singers and I knew that they needed to be a very high standard, therefore I brought in someone to help me organise the technical side of the music for the band. He was much better technically than me and at the time also much more experienced at worship leading. However, I will never forget his response. He said to me, "Vanessa, you are called to lead this and therefore God has given you the blueprint. Therefore I will submit to you and support you." Wow! I was blown away by his humility and heart to support me. But I learnt something from him that day – God gives the plan and the blueprint to the one who is leading. All the rest of us need to get behind and support the leader and so bring the unity and the blessing of the Lord.

Have you ever looked into the sky and seen large birds flying in a 'V' formation? Every autumn hundreds of geese fly over our house in the morning and evening. It's an awesome sight. In particular, scientists have been studying the Ibis as they fly in the 'V' formation and why they do this. Their study has revealed that these big-winged birds carefully position their wing tips and synchronise their flapping to catch the preceding bird's updraft, and thereby save energy during flight. Also after a while the front bird, which is doing the most work, will then go to the back and another will take its place at the front.

What a fantastic example of the power of unity! In the same way we need to get behind our leaders, for together, in unity there is no limit to what we can achieve.

They were responsible for the development of others

For a moment, try to imagine the whole picture of the numbers in the Tabernacle.

King David was the leader or Senior Pastor. Under him was Chenaniah the Chief Musician who was in charge of the whole music ministry. Under Chenaniah were the three worship leaders: Asaph had four sons, Heman had fourteen sons and Jeduthun had six sons. They were then responsible for 288 singers.

> *So the number of them, with their brethren who were instructed in the songs of the Lord, all who were skilful, was two hundred and eighty-eight.*

> *1 Chronicles 25:7*

And then the whole body of student musicians and singers were 4000.

> ...*Four thousand praised the Lord with musical instruments, "which I made," said David, "for giving praise."*

> *1 Chronicles 23:5*

Wow! Can you imagine organising such a large number?

The lesson we learn here, however, is that it is always God's heart for us to disciple and help in the development of others into the ministry. Never be afraid of building up others to take your place, because God will see your heart to disciple others and then in turn He will promote you. In fact, whenever we promote others we promote ourselves.

They cast lots for their duty

> *And he appointed some of the Levites to minister before the ark of the* LORD, *to commemorate, to thank, and to praise the* LORD *God of Israel.*

> *1 Chronicles 16:4*

Soon after God called me to the ministry, Bruce McGrail came to Kensington Temple. Bruce was a Chief Musician and his ministry was to teach and set up music ministries in churches all over the world. I was a young Christian, this was my calling, and I was like a sponge soaking up all the teaching. Bruce imparted to me a great deal and I was greatly impacted by the way he encouraged a spirit of excellence in us all concerning the music ministry. His standard was very high. Everybody in the team was re-auditioned and he rebuilt the team from scratch. When he auditioned me I performed badly on the piano (my playing was terrible in those days), but thank God, Bruce was a godly man and he prayed about all of us. He said to me that God had spoken to him about me and that one day "I would be a great blessing to the Body of Christ!"

I was invited to join the team. Bruce mixed all the teams up: the small with the great, and teacher with the student according to God's word. No elite teams! No A team and B team and rubbish team!

I was put on the synthesiser, which was a backing instrument, often with Bruce leading on piano at the main 11am service, which was the most popular service. This was quite a baptism for me but gradually I built up confidence. Often, I was sure that my synth wasn't even plugged in but I learnt a valuable lesson that my worship was first and foremost unto God.

The teams in David's day ministered before the Lord day and night

There was no one singing along with them, cheering them on, just them and God. This is the heart of our calling. Our ministry is always first and foremost unto God whether we are at home or whether we are ministering before thousands of people.

The Warrior Bride

8

Worship Leading – the Journey of Worship

Therefore, I urge you, brothers, in view of God's mercy, to offer your bodies as living sacrifices, holy and pleasing to God – this is your spiritual act of worship.

Romans 12:1 (NIV)

Worship is a lifestyle

To be an effective worship leader it's important to be a worshipper at home. We will never be able to lead the congregation beyond our own experience. Do we hunger after God for more of Him and feed on His Word? We can't be a Sunday morning worshipper only; it will soon show in our worship leading. I believe the best worship leader is someone who loves to worship and is so inspirational in their own worship that we inspire others to worship too.

Worship leading is like piloting a plane. Have you ever looked at a Jumbo Jet weighing 300–400 tons and wondered how it was ever going to take off? I still don't know how it happens! All I know is that we speed down the runway and as we lift off another law kicks in; the law of aerodynamics. Then we ascend through the sky and arrive above the clouds into a permanent blue sky where the sun is always shining! Well it is similar when leading worship.

Sometimes I look at the congregation and wonder how is this ever going to take off! People coming from all over the place, chatting to each other, some people are down, some have had a good week, and some haven't even arrived yet. I usually start with a declaration to gather the people and then we are off, hurtling down the runway of praise! We gather momentum and people start engaging with Jesus, we feel the atmosphere start to change, praise is rising and then a different law kicks in *"For the law of the Spirit of life in Christ Jesus has made me free from the law of sin and death,"* *(Romans 8:2)* and we have lift off!

We feel the presence of the Lord increase; we are ascending into the spirit realm. We are arising in praise; we break through the clouds and enter into a different realm – the realm of the Spirit and realm of His glory. Here we have clear vision, here we encounter His presence, here we can hear from heaven. Here things change and our problems seem to disappear in His glorious presence, wrapped up in His love. We can hear His voice bringing words of life, healing and breakthrough. Here we are free to duck and dive and soar with the Spirit. Oh what a joy! We want to stay here forever…

We rest, we worship, we listen, we soak, we love Him and He is passionate about us. And now we have encountered Him, everything has changed. What was I so worried about before? Our enemy distorts everything, making mountains out of molehills. When we arise in praise corporately and in unity nothing can stand against us.

I'm always praying that God will prepare me for the next time of ministry. I am always asking God for new songs, the songs that reflect His heart. I also ask God for His sound when we minister in different meetings. The best worship service is going on in heaven and we need to be asking God to bring His sound to earth, *"on earth as it is in heaven"*. That is always my prayer when I minister; Lord let me bring your sound to earth, download your sounds to me today. A lady said to me one day, "Rather than downloading *iTunes* we want to download God's sounds!" I really agree with that statement.

Seeking God's heart

As we seek the Lord for His heart, we can expect to receive His blueprint and have some understanding in advance of what God is going to do. I believe that there are always key songs for a time of ministry. Songs that will be a springboard into the heart of God for that day. Of course, there is always room for God to move in unexpected ways and in different directions if He so wants or directs.

As a worship leader we need to be ready

If we are an instrumentalist, it's important to practice so that we are not worrying about practicalities on the day. If we are ministering with a band, it is helpful to be well rehearsed and practiced. There is much to think about when leading worship; we don't want to be worrying about technicalities when we minister.

Our first priority is to worship God, to listen to and follow the leading of the Holy Spirit

> *A fire shall always be burning on the altar; it shall never go out.*

> *Leviticus 6:13*

The Levites in the Old Testament would minister to God day and night without anyone supporting or singing with them. That was their main calling and task. When we lead worship, our main focus is to listen and follow the Holy Spirit. He is the chief worship leader and He knows the way to the heart of God and to the river of God.

Our second priority is to lead the congregation into the presence of God

Awareness of the congregation and connecting with them is important if we are to take them on a journey. It's important not to talk too much as the people want to worship and not be interrupted after every song with some exhortation. I remember being at a service where the worship leader went on for about twenty minutes, I thought we would never be able to worship! On the other hand, it's good to encourage the congregation at the beginning either with a testimony, a story, a prayer, an appropriate poem, a scripture or some other way.

One good way to start is with a declaration. I have a couple of very powerful declarations regarding what the Blood of Jesus has done for us. Not only does a declaration about the power of the blood encourage the one making the proclamation; declaring the power of the blood cleanses the atmosphere, liberates from any feelings of guilt and releases a spirit of worship.

Remember Asaph, one of David's chief worship leaders; his name means 'gatherer' and 'remover of reproach'. That is our job – to gather the people and to encourage them to worship. It's important that we lead from a place of victory and love. We don't know what people have walked through during their week. It's important that we don't beat them over the head if they are not worshipping as we think they should. The enemy is the accuser and pours condemnation over us; we are the ones who encourage and remove the reproach of the enemy.

Our third priority is to lead the band

If we work with a band, we need to have good communication and hand signals so that the band knows where we are going and can follow us. If we know the band well and practice regularly it makes life so much easier as they will learn to follow our signals and even our body language. Make sure that they all have their eyes open too! It's very difficult to communicate with the singers who have their eyes tight shut!

Recognise your enemy – he is the accuser

Remember we have an enemy! The enemy hates us and hates praise. Lucifer was created to worship with pipes, strings and timbrels formed in his body. He was fashioned to be heaven's worship leader, but he fell when he tried to exalt himself above God. When we begin to worship, Satan's body still resonates with the sound of our worship, and he has to get away from our sound. He cannot stay in a place where God's people are worshipping so intently that he is shaken beyond measure (Isaiah 14 and Ezekiel 28).

We need to recognise the enemy. I love loud noisy praise! I have some great scriptures now to back this up, some of which I have mentioned in a different chapter. But for now, suffice to say that King David, when he brought the Ark of God back to Zion, did it to the sound of *Teruah,* which means 'to split the ear with sound', 'to praise God loudly', 'a shout of alarm, a battle cry', 'a shout of joy or victory'. Wonderful! I have discovered that when we praise God in this way, some people get quite offended and don't like it. Be assured, I don't want to give people earache, however I have come to understand that sometimes the sound of praise is rattling the religious spirit and there can be a reaction. This type of praise brings freedom, deliverance and healing. Praise God!

Be yourself!

Everybody is an individual which means we all bring a different anointing and revelation. God is creative; no two worship leaders are the same or carry the same anointing.

We are unique! Although we can be inspired by other worship leaders, we should never try to be like them. We should always aspire to be our unique self and be who God has called us to be.

I would like to suggest that there are different styles of worship leading

> *...And in the midst of the throne, and around the throne, were four living creatures full of eyes in front and in back. The first living creature was like a lion, the second living creature like a calf, the third living creature had a face like a man, and the fourth living creature was like a flying eagle.*
>
> *Revelation 4:6-7*

This scripture outlines four possible different types. The first is like a lion. This relates to the worship leader who is very authoritarian. They are the leaders that command us to worship! The second is like a calf, the worship leader who is very happy, bubbly and soft in their approach. The third worship leader is like a man. I believe that this is the worship leader who leads a congregation into the presence of the Lord through talking and exhorting the congregation. Lastly is the eagle. This is the worship leader who rises like the eagle and soars into the heavenlies trusting that everyone is soaring with them!

Which one do you relate to? Maybe none of them – that's ok!

What's important is that YOU ARE YOU!

The journey of worship and song choice

> *For the law of the Spirit of life in Christ Jesus has made me free from the law of sin and death.*
>
> *Romans 8:2*

Worship Leading – the Journey of Worship

Just recalling the picture of worship leading being like piloting a big jumbo jet. When we look at the plane we wonder how this plane could ever take off. Sometimes we wonder how the congregation will ever rise up and worship and soar together in the spirit.

One of the keys to effective worship leading is song choice. As worship leaders we need to have some idea where we are going and how we are going to get there. Songs are the springboards into the spirit realm. If we get the right song the congregation is lifted higher and higher, if we choose the wrong song the whole meeting plummets! If that happens however, don't panic! God is very gracious and can pick it up again with the right song.

When we are planning the set of songs there are a few things to take into account.

Firstly, what is the destination? Secondly, what songs are going to get us there? What are the keys of the songs? What is the theme of the songs?

Our destination depends on where the Holy Spirit wants to take us. He is the Chief Worship Leader and first and foremost we need to be sensitive and follow Him.

Remember our aim is to lift the congregation through our encouragement and song choice so we can ascend with the Holy Spirit in the spiritual realm. We need to build a platform for the Holy Spirit, ever ascending into higher heights, like the plane above the clouds. We are creating the atmosphere for worship and gathering everyone with us so that we can ascend together in unity. When we choose a song it's important to understand that songs have different qualities of spirit, and we need to be sensitive to what songs flow together and cause us to ascend even higher. Also, the key is important, because if we drop the key, it can affect the worship.

It's good to maintain either the same key or to move up a key. If we drop a key, we need to work out a way to transition so the congregation does not notice. Remember, we are always building the atmosphere of worship. Another important point is never to stop the music, either piano or guitar, because when the music stops the atmosphere of worship is broken, unless it is one of those beautiful times when the Holy Spirit is hovering powerfully. Then it is right to be silent.

Being aware that songs have different qualities of spirit helps us to choose songs that flow together and take us on a journey into the very heart of God. There is a journey of worship. We start in a certain place and we finish in a different place. When we lead worship, we need to be aware of this journey so that we can flow with the Holy Spirit into the heart of God.

When we know that we are in the river of God and we sense the manifest presence of the Lord, then we flow with Him where He leads. If we have a long list of songs, we lay them down and listen to the Holy Spirit. We don't have to play all the songs. We can stay on one song, that's ok, we can play music and not sing at all. Usually for a 30 minute set, two to three songs is sufficient. We can sing in tongues or flow spontaneously, singing the word of God or a prophetic song. There is no hurry. It is a delight to linger in the presence of God. When God comes we want to stay in the river.

If we go from songs of sweet worship, to celebration and back to deliverance – in and out, and up and down, nobody knows where they are. The Bible teaches us that we enter His gates with thanksgiving and His courts with praise.

> *Enter into His gates with thanksgiving,*
> *And into His courts with praise.*

Be thankful to Him, and bless His name.

Psalm 100:4

We enter His gates with thanksgiving and gratitude in our hearts for who Jesus is and what He has done. Being grateful to God is the key to entering His presence. We enter His courts with praise and exalt Jesus and lift Him up above everything else, releasing faith to Him. Worship is like 'son' bathing. We enter into the Most Holy Place through the veil on our face in adoration to Him. There we rest in His love and allow Him to speak to us, love us, restore us and fill us again with His glory.

I would like to show you two models that might help you in thinking through the song direction.

The first model: The Tabernacle

Plan of the Tabernacle

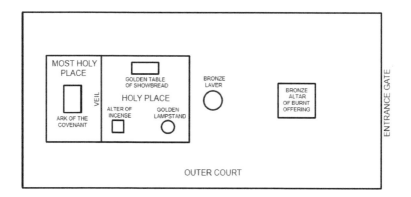

The Tabernacle is a shadow of Christ Himself and the sacrifice that He made for us. There are no formulas in our song choice, however these models can help us think through what is important. We don't need to incorporate every element suggested but it is good to be aware of them.

As we walk into the tabernacle there are different articles of furniture, which represent different aspects of our relationship with God as we make our way towards the Most Holy Place. As we approach God in our worship, we walk through the gates and the outer courts of the tabernacle into the Holy Place, through the veil and into the Most Holy Place. The Most Holy Place is always our destination. Remember, in the Old Testament only the High Priest could go into the Most Holy Place once a year and a rope would be tied around his feet so that if he died in the awesome presence, he could be pulled out.

Yet now, we have the amazing privilege of going into the Most Holy Place whenever and wherever we want because we are now the Tabernacle; our bodies are the Temple of the Holy Spirit. God's presence dwells within us! WOW! That is so awesome.

Imagine the congregation; they are coming through the gates into the outer court. We need some simple and easy rhythmic gathering songs. People come through the doors of the church; they are coming out of all sorts of different circumstances, saying hello to everyone, looking around the room, some are ready to worship, some may have had a difficult week. This is where we need some good gathering and thanksgiving songs. At this stage, imagine, we are taxiing towards the runway, gathering everyone together and preparing to go down the runway of praise and take off.

Having come through the gates into the outer court, the first article of furniture is the brazen altar. This is the place of sacrifice and represents the sacrifice of Jesus. Appropriate songs here are honouring and exalting Jesus. We always come through the cross, by faith and through His grace.

Next is the laver; this is a place of consecration and washing. We always need to be cleansed and washed by the blood of the Lamb. This could include a declaration on the blood, a prayer, a song or a scripture. Then we enter the Holy Place.

The articles of furniture are; the showbread which represents, the Word, the Bread of Life and God's provision, and the lampstand which represents the Holy Spirit (which in the Old Testament was quite a dim light). Therefore, when we approach God we know that we can be assured of His cleansing, His provision and the power of the Holy Spirit to breathe life and light into us.

The next article of furniture is the altar of incense. Our worship and our prayers come before God like incense. This is a place of fire, consecration and surrender. We go from here through the veil into the Most Holy Place. The attitude of our heart determines our position; on our face bowed down before Him. We need songs of the altar, songs that transition us from praise, through the veil, into His glory, into His heart and His manifest presence.

The Most Holy Place. This is a place of His power, of intimacy, of glory and of fire. We linger and wait in this place for His voice, His direction, His love and His enabling. Once in this place we do not want to move until the Holy Spirit leads. From this place we can move in different directions: sweet worship, grand worship, high praises or warfare. From here we enter a different realm in the Spirit. This is a place where we hear His voice. From here the spontaneous can be released and the prophetic can flow as heaven unfolds on earth.

The second model:

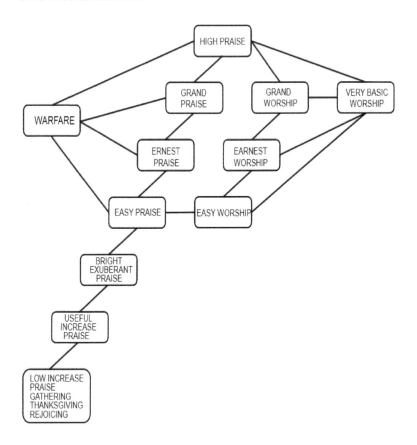

This classification is not so much that of choruses, but recognition of the different qualities of the spirit of the worship or praise. Songs can be listed under different headings only as a guide, so that when I interpret the character of the worship; its quality; its direction at any given moment, I can safely draw on those songs, expecting there to be a sustaining or an increase of that quality of spirit.

This second model looks rather strange; however it demonstrates different qualities of spirit in the songs and the flow of the Holy Spirit in different directions. You will notice that the songs start at the bottom with gathering, thanksgiving and rejoicing songs. As we move up the chart so does the intensity of increase in the Spirit. Praise songs become more earnest and bright and then the Holy Spirit can take us into grand praise or high praise or warfare, or into grand worship or sweet worship as mentioned before in the tabernacle song choices.

For example, if we feel that the Holy Spirit wants to take the service into warfare, then it is important to build the people into that place of intensity with good song choices. It is very difficult to drop straight into warfare. In fact, sometimes warfare can be even more dynamic and effective if the people rise up from a place of intimacy where they have really connected with the Father.

Here is an example of a good song list for a thirty-minute set just to illustrate, which I hope you find helpful.

The first song is an easy praise, gathering song. The keys flow either the same or rising. *Praise Is Rising* (*Hosanna*) (key G), the second song *This Is Amazing Grace* (key C) is a bright exuberant praise song, followed by *What A Beautiful Name It Is* (key D), an earnest worship song that takes you through the veil into the Most Holy Place, finishing with *For Thou Oh Lord* (key D) which can lead into grand worship.

Here is an example of a poor song list which illustrates lack of direction and flow. (Just to say I love all these songs, but just not together in this order!) For instance: *I Love You Lord* (key D) (soft easy worship), followed by a warfare song such as *There Is Power In The Name Of Jesus* (key B), followed by a bright praise song such as *In The River* (key F), followed by a song on the cross for example.

I would always encourage you to start your praise time with songs that focus on Jesus and His greatness rather than on 'me and my needs'. Often people come to church feeling down, they've had a difficult week, perhaps a difficult morning. When we start to look up to Him and His greatness and His grace, then we forget about ourselves, and we release our faith to Him. Often at the end of our time of worship we can't even see our problems as they have been reduced from a mountain to a molehill!

When we sing songs about the majesty and greatness of God, the revelation of His Majesty slips from our head to our heart and we find ourselves experiencing his Majesty as we walk into His throne room. Music and songs carry power and revelation. When we sing songs about his love and intimacy with Him, we experience His love as He touches our hearts and releases revelation that He is the lover of our souls. Worship is powerful and impacts our mind, our heart and our spirit in a profound way.

Tips on flowing with the Holy Spirit

At Home

- Worship leading always starts with our own relationship with God.
- Know the word of God; be immersed in His word.
- Meditate and memorise scripture.
- Pray in tongues regularly, so constantly tuning your spirit and aligning your heart to God.
- Worship on your musical instrument and get used to flowing with the Holy Spirit at home.
- Sing and play your own songs and practice improvising.
- Get right with God quickly; keep your heart right.

- Develop and build your intimacy with God and guard your prayer times with God, they are life.
- Soak in His presence.
- Practice technicalities to avoid worrying about them in the service.

Music Team Meetings

> *Behold, how good and how pleasant it is*
> *For brethren to dwell together in unity!*
> *It is like the precious oil upon the head,*
> *Running down on the beard,*
> *The beard of Aaron...*
> *For there the LORD commanded the blessing –*
> *life forevermore.*
>
> *Psalm 133*

- Music Team Meetings are very important, not just for learning new songs, but also for gathering together, building relationship, and worshipping together. We need to have confidence and trust in one another to enable us to take risks and step out into new things and not be afraid to make a mistake.
- Watch out for one another, pray for one another and ask for prayer cover from the leaders of the church. The enemy hates a music team that is in unity and moving forward in the things of God and will try to disrupt as much as possible. Be on the alert and aware of his tactics.
- Preserving the unity and relationships in the band is a top priority. The enemy will try and pick us off at our weakest points and thereby nullify the effect of the team.
- As the leader, be aware when the Holy Spirit is on the different team members. Maybe to play a solo; bring a

prophetic word; to bring a song; to exhort the congregation. The synergy of the team working together in unity and order brings a much more powerful anointing. It's important to have clear hand signals and communication lines to understand one another and give clear direction. All these things need to be discussed, understood and practiced in the music practice.

- Music practice is a good time to try out new things together, like singing scripture. You can take a scripture, for example a Psalm or a Revelation hymn, and sing it. Firstly, read through the Psalm and then one after the other sing a line from the Psalm and then go around again and sing a related thought. The Holy Spirit will lead you into fresh revelation and a very enjoyable and powerful time of worship together as a team.

- Sometimes just worship together in tongues and spontaneous singing and wait on the Lord in His presence.

- Practice prophesying over one another; develop your seeing, hearing or sensing what God is saying to one another.

- The more you seek God together, the more it will overflow into the services where you are ministering.

- Always follow your leader, even if you don't agree with where they are going. They have the blueprint and the authority to lead and it's important that the rest of the team press in behind the leader to preserve the unity of the team.

Leading Worship and Ministering

- Love God, not the performance. Engage with God and with the Holy Spirit.

- Lead from a place of victory and love; love the people.
- Be prepared for what God wants to do.
- Desire and have confidence to step out, remember we have the mind of Christ.
- It's a partnership with the Holy Spirit.
- We have the blueprint; the others should follow.
- We have God given authority.
- Don't be afraid of silence. Sometimes there are pregnant silences, which are wonderful, when discerned correctly.
- Encourage the congregation to physically move as this can facilitate a breakthrough in the spiritual realm. This could include clapping or dancing, even the simple raising of hands.
- Engaging with the congregation at the outset is so important. Maybe a scripture, a declaration, a testimony, an exhortation or a brief story.
- Remember the ebb and flow of the Holy Spirit is like waves breaking over us. There are times of high praises, times of quiet intimacy, times of silence and times of musical interlude.
- Watch the people, listen to God. Ask for revelation. When you are in the river, stay there for a while and trust the Holy Spirit. Don't move on too quickly. Wait on the Holy Spirit. When there is a lull then gently move on.
- Keep the music going all the time (even if very quietly) as the music sustains the anointing. A little word for the drummers: be sensitive how to end a chorus; just stopping abruptly can break the anointing. It may be right to continue sensitively or finish with a drum roll and crash of the cymbals. Whatever we do, we need to flow with the worship leader and the Holy Spirit.

- Sometimes there is a natural ascending of the Holy Spirit in the congregation, these times are precious and we should facilitate and flow with what God is doing. In these times, keep the music going quietly underneath. Keep the music simple.
- At the end of service, in the ministry time, try singing and reflecting in song on what has been preached, thereby affirming the message into the hearts of the congregation.
- Sometimes there is a natural ascending of the Holy Spirit on the team members. We need to be aware of that and encourage team members to step out.

9

The Dance of Intercession and Worship

Worship Leading and Flowing with Intercession

Does the eagle mount up at your command,
And make its nest on high?
On the rock it dwells and resides,
On the crag of the rock and the stronghold.
From there it spies out the prey;
Its eyes observe from afar.

Job 39:27-29

An eagle has an inborn ability to sense the motion of air currents. It often won't budge until the right breeze comes along. When it does, the eagle just lets go. Yes, it flaps its wings, but mostly the eagle just lets go, and is borne aloft on the wings of the wind. They have the ability to lock their wings and ride the wind effortlessly. What a beautiful picture of worship.

But those who wait on the LORD
Shall renew their strength;
They shall mount up with wings like eagles,
They shall run and not be weary,
They shall walk and not faint.

Isaiah 40:31

We are like eagles. We wait for the Holy Spirit and then we ride on the thermals of God's Spirit and we rise higher and higher effortlessly and with grace. Then from the heights of the rock where the eagle dwells, it watches, waits and spies out its prey. An eagle can see what other birds do not see hence the expression 'an eagle's eye view'. They can see a tiny lizard on a rock at a thousand feet. They can see the movement of a fish underwater. An eagle has the ability to know when a storm is coming and when the storm hits, it sets its wings so that the wind will pick it up and lift it above the storm. While the storm rages below, the eagle is soaring above it. The eagle does not escape the storm. It simply uses the storm to lift it higher. It rises on the winds that bring the storm.

In the same way worship and intercession work together beautifully

We rise in worship on eagles' wings above the storm, using songs exalting His greatness, that take us up and out of our small view, into the grandeur and majesty of God. From that place of authority, God anoints our eyes to see and then releases revelation and understanding how to pray, to bring breakthrough and establish His will. Then with absolute precision we can swoop down on our prey and execute His written judgement; for example healing to the sick, freedom to the prisoner, unity where there is disunity, healing to our land, etc.

> *Let the high praises of God be in their mouth,*
> *And a two-edged sword in their hand,*
> *To execute vengeance on the nations,*
> *And punishments on the peoples;*
> *To bind their kings with chains,*
> *And their nobles with fetters of iron;*
> *To execute on them the written judgment –*

The Dance of Intercession and Worship

This honour have all His saints.

Psalm 149:6-9

Like the eagle, when we flow on the thermals of His Spirit, there is an ease and a joy about prayer. Then we rise again to worship Him on the thermals of His love and we are refreshed. It's so important to keep our focus on Him. And from that place we wait for Him for the next revelation and direction from heaven of what to pray and how to pray.

This is the dance of worship and prayer

It is easy and refreshing moving with the ebb and flow on His Spirit.

Remember to keep the music going throughout the prayer. The music sustains the anointing; when we stop the music, the anointing drops. But we need to be sensitive as to what to play on our instrument. A gentle string or pad sound on the keyboard is a wonderful sound that sustains and undergirds the prayer. Nothing too loud or intrusive. However, if the prayer becomes militant and aggressive the music should reflect the mood of the prayer. When we reflect the prayer in music it enhances the sound and supports the intercessor.

The Warrior Bride

10

Harp and Bowl
Singing and Praying Scripture
Singing Spontaneously and Developing the Prophetic Flow

Now when He had taken the scroll, the four living creatures and the twenty-four elders fell down before the Lamb, each having a harp, and golden bowls full of incense, which are the prayers of the saints.

Revelation 5:8

When we first stepped out into our ministry, *Liberation Ministries,* in 1999, we had the opportunity to visit the 'International House of Prayer' in Kansas City under the leadership of Mike Bickle. This is a 24/7 prayer furnace in the Spirit of the Tabernacle of David, the home of the 'Harp and Bowl' Ministry which is a model for 24/7 worship and prayer, where the worship never stops. IHOP have been running with this vision now for well over 25 years and inspiring houses of prayer all over the world.

When we went to Kansas, God had already been showing me the joy of flowing spontaneously in the Spirit by singing scripture. The ministry of 'Harp and Bowl' greatly impacted me. I loved the team ministry and the model which releases the spontaneity and the free flow of the Holy Spirit while singing and expounding scripture.

I was particularly touched by one session when some of the singers were singing and developing a theme from the *Song of*

Songs. What was touching and beautiful was the depth of the revelation as they sang for two hours from *Song of Songs 1:2-3*.

> *Let him kiss me with the kisses of his mouth*
> *For your love is better than wine.*
> *Because of the fragrance of your good ointments,*
> *Your name is ointment poured forth.*

They went backwards and forward, one after the other, questioning, responding and opening up truths from the scripture all in song. It was dynamic!

> *Let the word of Christ dwell in you richly in all wisdom, teaching and admonishing one another in Psalms and hymns and spiritual songs, singing with grace in your hearts to the Lord.*
>
> *Colossians 3:16*

What is the spirit of the tabernacle of David?

Because of David's type of New Testament relationship with God, the tabernacle was open to all to come and worship before the Lord. There was continual worship and music according to God's direction. David had a team of 4000 musicians and singers. The teams would minister to the Lord day and night and sing antiphonally and responsively to one another.

> *And the heads of the Levites were Hashabiah, Sherebiah, and Jeshua the son of Kadmiel, with their brothers across from them, to praise and give thanks, group alternating with group, according to the command of David the man of God.*
>
> *Nehemiah 12:24*

Antiphonal singing

'Antiphonal music is that performed by two choirs in interaction, often singing alternate musical phrases. Antiphonal psalmody is the singing or musical playing of psalms by alternating groups of performers'.

David understood the movement and antiphonal sound in heaven.

The Tabernacle was where music flowed freely; the song of the Lord would go back and forth between the choirs in the tent. It was free flowing, it was fluid and it was spontaneous, it was alive and exciting.

They proclaimed the word of the Lord in song. Many of the Psalms were written for antiphonal singing. For example, *Psalm 136 'Your love endures forever'* punctuates every other line in this Psalm. One group would sing a line and the other group would respond with *'Your love endures forever'*.

> *Give thanks to the Lord, for He is good!*
> *For His mercy endures forever.*
> *Oh, give thanks to the God of gods!*
> *For His mercy endures forever.*
> *Oh, give thanks to the Lord of lords!*
> *For His mercy endures forever:*
> *To Him who alone does great wonders,*
> *For His mercy endures forever;*
> *To Him who by wisdom made the heavens,*
> *For His mercy endures forever;*

Psalm 136:1-5

Psalm 24 is another example of a Psalm written for antiphonal singing:

Question: *'Who is this King of glory?'*

The Warrior Bride

Response: 'The Lord strong and mighty.'

> *Lift up your heads, O you gates!*
> *And be lifted up, you everlasting doors!*
> *And the King of glory shall come in.*
> *Who is this King of glory?*
> *The Lord strong and mighty,*
> *The Lord mighty in battle.*

Psalm 24:7-8

There is movement in heaven, it is not a monologue; it is a dialogue, things are happening, it is not static! When we lead worship, our desire is always to hear the sound of heaven, move with it and bring it to earth, as David did.

Harp and Bowl is the dance of worship and intercession; the harp is the worship and the bowl is the prayer of the saints. The Harp and Bowl model consists of a prayer leader, a worship leader and prophetic singers.

In a typical cycle of apostolic intercessory prayer, the worship leader leads a couple of songs and then leads into a spontaneous time of worship where everyone sings in tongues or a spontaneous song to stir up their spirits and align themselves with the Spirit of God and to release the free flow of the heart.

Then the prayer leader announces the prayer topic and the scripture. The scripture is read and the prayer leader starts praying into the chosen subject. At the end of the prayer, the intercessor finishes with *'In Jesus' Name'* as a signal to the singers that he has finished, the prophetic singers then take up the prayer in song. One after the other they develop the prayer and the theme in song using the scripture that has been brought by the prayer leader. The song gives wings to the prayer as it is lifted to the throne of God.

Added to that is the chorus leader, who leads simple refrains that punctuate the singing, where everyone can join in. This is a great way to regather everybody through the cycle. The prayer leader then prays again into the same subject and the singers once again lift the prayer to God in song, one after the other, proclaiming and declaring the word in song. This pattern is repeated until the Holy Spirit gives a release to end the cycle.

While this is happening, there is a flow in the Spirit that takes place and the prayer leader, worship leader, singers and congregation go on a wonderful journey with the Holy Spirit into the heart of God concerning that topic. Revelation and a prophetic flow are released as they follow the leading of the Spirit. A typical cycle can go on for about twenty minutes just praying for the same topic. This is the dance of worship and intercession.

It is the most liberating and exhilarating way to pray for two hours. God wants us to enjoy praying in His House.

> *Even them I will bring to My holy mountain,*
> *And make them joyful in My house of prayer.*
>
> *Isaiah 56:7*

Spontaneous singing; singing in the spirit and singing the scripture

Developing the flow of the spirit outside the box of choruses

> *For if I pray in a tongue, my spirit prays, but my understanding is unfruitful. What is the conclusion then? I will pray with the spirit, and I will also pray with the understanding. I will sing with the spirit, and I will also sing with the understanding.*
>
> *1 Corinthians 14:14-15*

Worship is about developing a free flowing, spontaneous song of the heart. It is the song that you make up as you go along.

I recall the first time I sang spontaneously. I was at home with some friends and we were worshipping together. I was a young Christian exploring the things of God. As we worshipped I started singing out to God my own love song. I will never forget it! I felt so free; it was wonderful to feel my spirit soar with the Holy Spirit.

Singing spontaneously, whether in tongues or your own song, releases faith and intensity to encounter the manifest presence of God. It opens the human heart to the Holy Spirit in an enhanced way. I have found that singing scripture is a spring board to singing spontaneously and then prophetically. It is a most wonderful way to develop the prophetic song in a way that is safe and accurate while at the same time experiencing the exhilaration of partnering with the Holy Spirit.

I encourage you to pick a scripture, preferably to start with a Psalm or Revelation hymn for example

> *Holy, holy, holy,*
> *Lord God Almighty,*
> *Who was and is and is to come!*

Revelation 4:8

Read it through; sing it through; then take it line by line repeating lines when you feel the life of the Spirit. If you can accompany yourself on guitar or piano, keep the chords underneath very simple just to undergird your song. Then stay with the line that impacts you and start developing it with related thoughts and you will find that the Holy Spirit will take you on a journey into the heart of God and release to you a 'now' word into your spirit for that day.

This is how we can develop new songs. You can do this with someone else too. Take it in turns to sing a line, one after the other, and experience the thrill of the journey with the Holy Spirit.

Singing and Praying in Tongues

> *I wish you all spoke with tongues.*
>
> *1 Corinthians 14:5*

> *Likewise the Spirit also helps in our weaknesses. For we do not know what we should pray for as we ought, but the Spirit Himself makes intercession for us with groanings which cannot be uttered.*
>
> *Romans 8:26*

Part of developing a flowing heart and singing spontaneously, is singing and praying in tongues. When we pray and sing in tongues we are tuning our vocal instrument to the Spirit of God. It is a bit like tuning a violin, cello or guitar. We are aligning ourselves with heaven and as we pray and sing we receive revelation and download from heaven. Sometimes, when we don't know how to pray, we can pray and sing in tongues and then receive revelation about how to pray God's will into that situation. We know that we are releasing God's power and praying His perfect will, even though sometimes we don't know what we are praying.

Do you want your heart to burn within you?

Let the Living Word open up the written word to you:

> *And they said to one another, "Did not our heart burn within us while He talked with us on the road, and while He opened the Scriptures to us?"*
>
> *Luke 24:32*

After His crucifixion Jesus walked with His disciples on the road to Emmaus and explained what was going on. He unfolded the scriptures to them and they said that their hearts burned within them. This is the experience you will have as you unfold the scripture with the help and guidance of the Holy Spirit.

Below I have outlined some of the benefits of singing the scriptures rather than just reading them, it is much more challenging to sing them, as it requires more of our attention!

1. When we sing the Word of God, it requires us to vocalise our prayers. It is a remedy to wandering thoughts! It slows our hearts and mind to the necessary pace to digest the truth. We have to quieten our soul. Some of us find it very difficult to quieten our souls in prayer. There are so many distractions and so many things to do. We can gabble spoken prayers and we can do it without thinking, but we can't sing the Word fast and if we are not concentrating we lose our focus and quit singing.

2. Singing scripture opens the emotions; the musical factor of singing opens the chambers of the heart. It is a mystery. God made us in His image and He is musical. Music reaches us like nothing else; it opens something in our hearts.

3. We can pray, we can speak in tongues, however, when we start to sing in tongues and sing the scripture, it opens something in our hearts and what was head knowledge slips into our hearts as we sing and receive revelation of the Word we are singing. We start to receive understanding into our hearts like never before. External music is

powerful; however internal music has far greater impact.

4. There is a discipleship factor in that we are studying the Word of God and allowing the Word to impact our lives. It personalises the Word to us. We are our own best teacher and when we sing the Word the Holy Spirit downloads fresh revelation to us. As we continue to sing out the revelation that He gives to us, the Holy Spirit takes us on our own personal journey with Him.

5. New songs are birthed out of singing the Word.

6. As we sing and learn scripture and expound the Word in song we are developing a new love language of the heart which takes us beyond 'Praise the Lord' and 'Hallelujah'.

Head knowledge becomes heart knowledge as we sing scripture

Worthy is the Lamb who was slain
To receive power and riches and wisdom,
And strength and honour and glory and
blessing!

Revelation 5:12

As we sing the Revelation songs about His Majesty, we start to experience and receive revelation of His greatness and our hearts are impacted. Instead of looking inwards at ourselves we are lifted up as we gaze on His greatness. This is a great place to start when involved in intercession, as we start to see things from His perspective rather than ours.

Equally, when we sing *Song of Songs* or any intimate scriptures we start to enter into the revelation that Jesus is the lover of our soul and He draws us into intimacy. These revelations are very healing and life changing as we gaze upon His face and His love for us. I recommend studying *Song of Songs* and memorising some of it, thereby increasing your vocabulary in your worship so you can sing it freely and enter into that intimacy with Him.

Finally, this ability to flow with the spirit has to be developed and nurtured. We have to cultivate a spontaneous heart and a prophetic spirit that flows like a river inside us. I encourage you to start singing scripture and developing a spontaneous heart and experience the exhilaration of flowing with the revelation of heaven.

I trust that this book has been a blessing to you, not only to lift your vision as to where you are going in your worship and your relationship with God, but also given you practical ways, to achieve a free flowing spontaneous heart in worship, and to partner with the Holy Spirit in the journey.

Books and Resources from Brian and Vanessa Richardson

Don't Quit Now! Go For Your Dreams

By Brian and Vanessa Richardson

From his rich experience of well over 50 years of ministry in many parts of the world, Brian shares in this book some important principles in life – with more than a sprinkling humour – that have helped keep him on track living the Kingdom life.

Vanessa too tells something of her story and how she has held on to her God-given dreams until, by God's grace, they became a reality.

Brian and Vanessa Richardson

Brian and Vanessa were married in 1993 and have a daughter Anna. They launched Liberation Ministries in October 1999 and since then have ministered in conferences and churches in the UK, Arab Emirates, South America, USA, India, Europe and Eastern Europe.

Now You Do It!
A Challenge to Plant New Churches
By Brian Richardson

The heart of this book is to challenge mature Christians and congregations to church plant. It is also designed to encourage and give direction to those who may be considering the possibilities of church planting, to go for it!

It takes you on a journey from why we need to open new churches, to the actual launching of a bouncing baby church. On the way, we take a realistic look at our own potential, and then follow the process of conception to birth of a new church.

Spicing the story with humour, Brian shares from his own personal experience and that of the London City Church (that has planted more than 150 congregations over a 15 year period), the different models that can be undertaken.

Also available in French and Bulgarian.

Commendations:

Brian writes not from theory, but as one who has 'done it' and can draw on a wealth of experience from the UK and around the world.

Norman Barnes
Links International

I commend this book which shares vital concepts in a readable and practical style.

John Glass, Former General Superintendent, Elim
Pentecostal Church

The Dance by Vanessa Richardson

This CD takes you on a dance from high praise to the very heart of God and then on to being part of His Warrior Bride.

There are songs of intimate worship and aggressive praise where you can sing along with Vanessa and her excellent band.

BREAKOUT!

An Instrumental Album by Vanessa Richardson

The words of scripture have the wonderful ability to turn our lives around, set us free and lead us into our true destiny.

In this CD Vanessa seeks to interpret on the keyboard, backed by guitar and percussion, specific passages of scripture to take us on a journey through music and touch our spirits in a different way.

Your Kingdom Come
The Now And The Not Yet!

By Brian Richardson

A look at the Kingdom of Solomon and how it foreshadows the Kingdom of Christ.

'Your Kingdom come, Your will be done on earth as it is in heaven,' Matthew 6:10.

What do we expect to see when we pray 'Your Kingdom come?'

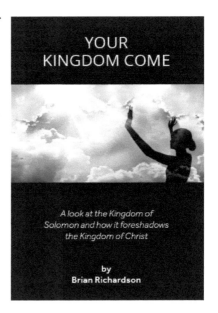

Commendation

Like a rich tapestry this book weaves wisdom, insight, research, illustration and humour to depict and vital subject. The author known to me for many years writes out of rich and authentic experience as a pastor of pastors. I commend it to you.

Rev John Glass
Chair of Council – Evangelical Alliance
Former General Superintendent of Elim Church

All resources are available to buy from
www.liberationministries.co.uk